**Welcome to Loo a
Your Time to S
Beauty, Self-Care, W(
Relaxation, and Christmas Activities!**

Take a quick escape with lighthearted reads, holiday-themed humor, beauty tips, and simple wellness ideas designed to bring a smile to your face. Perfect for those in-between moments, this book is packed with festive cheer and fun activities to brighten your day, wherever you are.

Table of Contents

1. **Laughter for Every Occasion**
2. **Beauty Secrets Without the Filter**
3. **Wellness Tips for the Busy Woman**
4. **Everyday Dilemmas (and How to Deal with Them)**
5. **Fun Facts to Amaze and Amuse**
6. **Positive Thoughts for a Quick Break**
7. **Just for Laughs – Quizzes and Mini-Tests**
8. **Self-Care Ideas for Every Mood**
9. **The Power of Positive Habits**
10. **Holiday Word Search**
11. **Christmas Sudoku**
12. **Holiday Seek & Find**

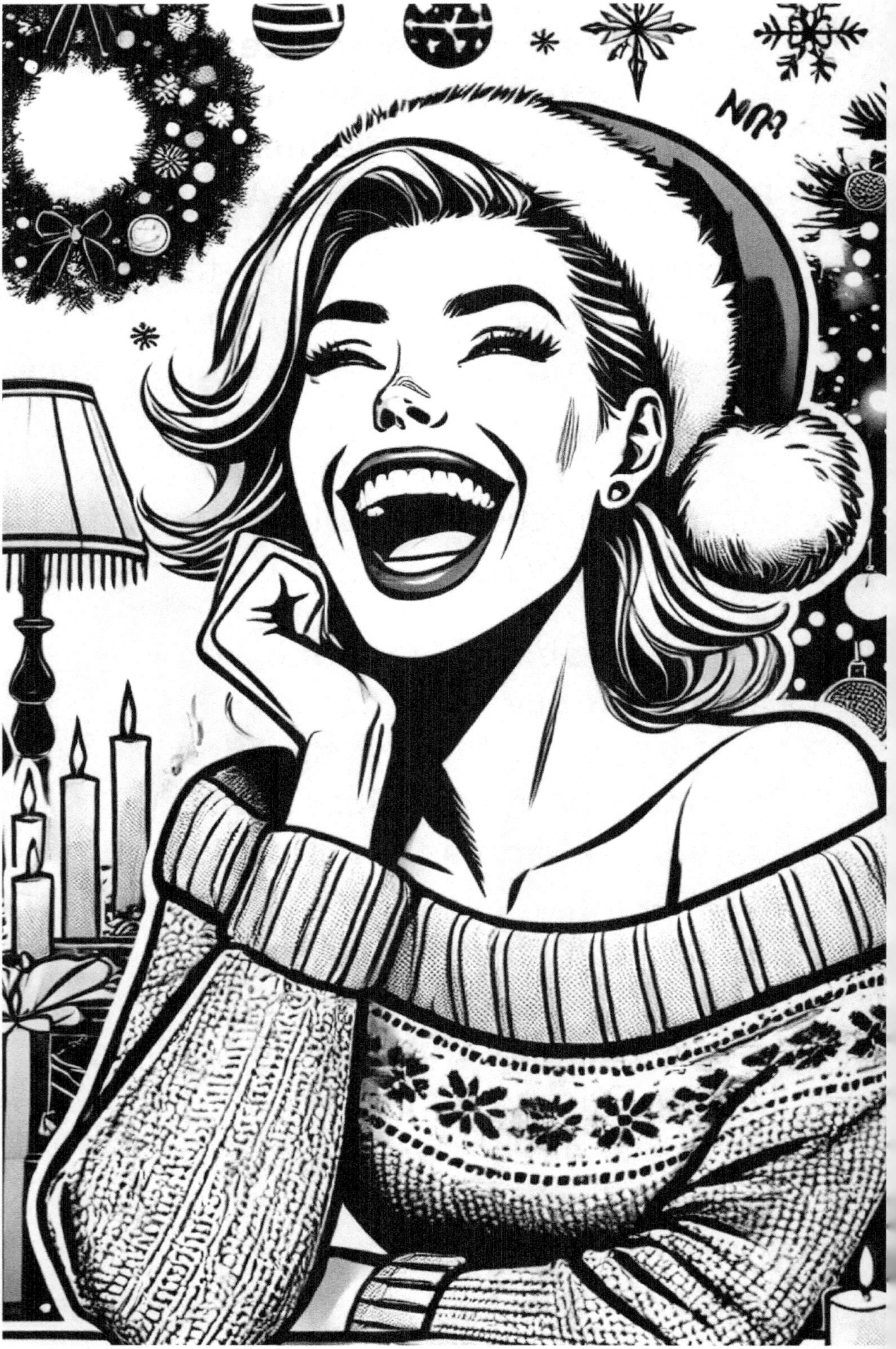

Chapter 1: Laughter for Every Occasion

Laughter connects us. It's the universal language that lifts moods, eases tension, and makes even the most ordinary moments extraordinary. This chapter is a deep dive into the science, fun, and little-known benefits of laughter, plus a collection of jokes and anecdotes designed to make you chuckle wherever you are.

The Benefits of a Good Laugh

Laughter doesn't just make us feel good – it's proven to have lasting health benefits! Let's explore some surprising ways laughter impacts our well-being.

Laughter as Exercise:

Did you know that laughing for just 10–15 minutes can burn up to 40 calories? That's roughly the same as taking a light walk! So, while laughter may not replace your gym routine, it adds a bonus calorie burn. Just think of it as a little workout you can do anywhere!

Mental Boost:
Laughter releases endorphins, those "feel-good" hormones, reducing stress and making us feel happier overall. Studies show that people who laugh more frequently experience lower levels of stress, anxiety, and even depression.

Immune Power-Up:
When you laugh, your body increases its production of antibodies, which strengthen the immune system. In other words, a hearty laugh might just help keep the sniffles away!

Pain Relief:
The endorphins released during laughter also act as natural painkillers. This is why people often feel better – even physically – after a good laugh.

Social Glue:
Laughter bonds people together. When we laugh with others, our brains release oxytocin, a hormone that promotes social bonding and feelings of trust. This is why shared laughter can make friendships and family bonds even stronger.

Laughing Through the Ages: Fun Facts

Ancient Laughter:
Laughter isn't just a modern pastime! The ancient Greeks believed in "laughing clubs," where people would gather just to laugh together. This was one of the first forms of laughter therapy!

Laughing Animals?
Believe it or not, humans aren't the only ones who laugh. Research shows that animals like chimpanzees, rats, and even some birds have sounds and behaviors that resemble laughter!

Babies Know Best:
Did you know that babies laugh about 300 times a day, while adults laugh only around 20 times? Perhaps we could all use a little more childlike joy in our lives.

Jokes for Any Moment

And now, for the real fun! Here are some jokes to make you laugh wherever you are. Try one on a friend, or just enjoy it yourself – laughter is always better when shared!

Why did I start a new diet? **To have something to cheat on every Friday night.**

My new fitness goal? **Walk down one aisle in Target without buying a candle.**

Why did the coffee date never work out? **He was a decaf guy, and I'm all espresso.**

Finally found my spirit animal: **She sleeps 10 hours a night and cancels plans.**

What's my idea of multitasking? **Browsing online shops while pretending to clean.**

I went to the gym today. **– Said no one who found a good sale online.**

Why did I cancel plans last minute? **My sweatpants and I had a "Netflix and chill" agreement.**

They say money can't buy happiness,
but have they seen my shoe collection?

My idea of meal prep:
Choosing between takeout and delivery.

You know you're an adult when... **you have a favorite spatula and nobody better touch it.**

Why did I break up with my diet?
It was too high-maintenance.

I run on three things: **Coffee, dry shampoo, and "I'll be there in five!"**

Why did I refuse to buy more Tupperware?
Because none of them have lids, and it's a mystery every time.

What's my daily skincare routine?
Step 1: Start. Step 2: Forget halfway.

Why did I skip my workout? **My yoga mat looked too comfortable to leave.**

Quick Anecdotes to Brighten Your Day

Sometimes, a short story can deliver as much laughter as a joke. Here are some real-life funny moments to remind you that humor can be found in the everyday:

The Grocery List Fail:

One woman texted her husband a list that said, "Pick up broccoli, cheese, and eggs, please!" He came home with a strange look and handed her one piece of broccoli, a block of cheese, and one single egg. Turns out he thought she meant only one of each. That dinner was a little less filling than planned!

The Pet Trick:

A dog owner tried teaching his new puppy to fetch. He tossed the toy across the room, expecting an enthusiastic fetch. The puppy watched the toy go, turned to his owner, yawned, and laid down to nap instead. Lesson learned – not all dogs have a natural calling for fetch!

In Closing: Laughter is a gift, and it's free! From funny stories to shared laughs, let's brighten each day. Life is short – embrace the humor in every moment!

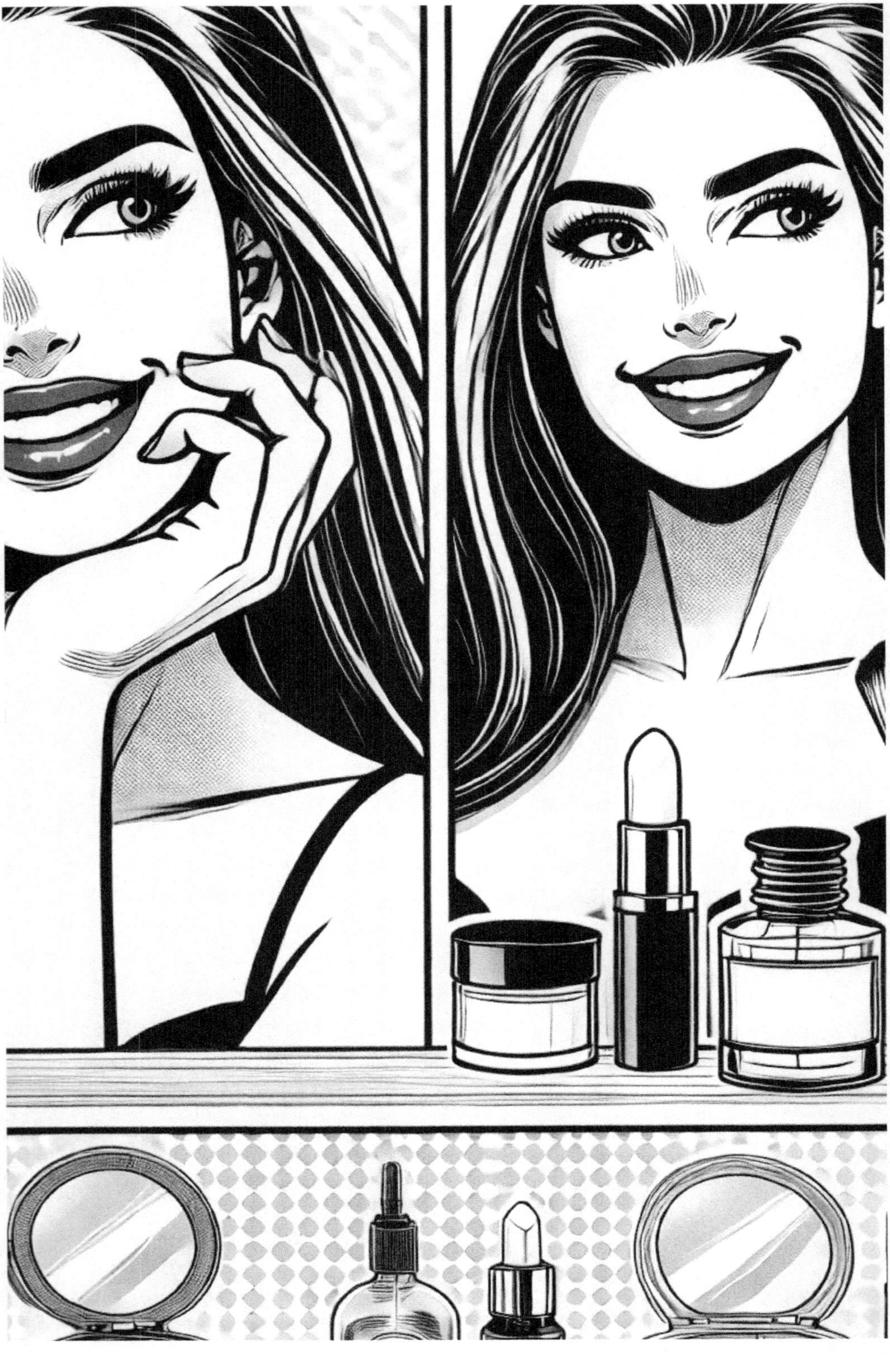

Chapter 2: Beauty Secrets Without the Filter

In a world filled with filters, beauty can often seem unattainable or over-the-top. But real beauty isn't about perfection; it's about feeling good in your own skin and embracing what makes you unique. This chapter is here to celebrate fun, authentic beauty tips, from simple hacks to mood-boosting routines, plus a few funny moments in makeup that remind us all – beauty doesn't have to be serious!

Beauty Hack Heaven:
Simple Tips for Every Day

Who doesn't love a quick and easy beauty trick? These tips are designed to make your routine simpler, faster, and just a little more fun!

The Ice Water Wake-Up:

For puffy eyes or tired skin in the morning, try dunking your face in a bowl of cold water for a few seconds. It's like an instant face-lift, and it wakes you up in no time! Added bonus: you'll feel extra fresh, like you're prepping for a magazine shoot – even if it's just for another Zoom call.

Lipstick as Blush:
In a hurry? Dab a bit of your lipstick on your cheeks for a quick blush. It's a fast way to add a pop of color, and it means fewer products to carry in your bag. Just make sure the shade works for both!

The Teaspoon Trick:
Need a quick eyelash curl? Heat a teaspoon in warm water, dry it off, and gently press it against your lashes. This trick works like a lash curler in a pinch – just test the temperature first!

Dry Shampoo Hack:
Dry shampoo can be a lifesaver, but for a quicker, budget-friendly option, use a bit of baby powder at the roots to soak up excess oil. Plus, it's great for creating texture and volume if you're after that beachy look.

Instant Highlighter with Lotion:
If you're after a natural glow, mix a tiny bit of lotion with a dab of highlighter and apply it to your cheekbones, brow bones, and collarbone. It'll give you a beautiful glow that says, "I woke up like this."

Mood-Boosting Beauty Routines

Sometimes, beauty isn't just about how you look; it's about how you feel. Here are some easy ways to make your daily routine more uplifting.

The Five-Minute Spa:

Turn an ordinary shower into a spa moment by adding a few drops of essential oil (like eucalyptus or lavender) to the shower walls before you step in. The steam will create a calming aroma that soothes you instantly – and the mini-luxury is a little treat for your mind.

DIY Facial Massage:

Take a minute to give yourself a quick facial massage before bed. Use gentle upward strokes around the cheeks, jawline, and forehead. It helps release tension, promotes circulation, and honestly, it just feels amazing. Plus, you'll wake up with a fresh, glowing face!

Color Psychology:
Did you know colors can affect your mood? Use this to your advantage with your nail polish or makeup shades. Bright colors like coral and pink are known to boost mood, while blues and greens can be calming. Play around with your look depending on how you want to feel that day!

Smile Therapy:
Believe it or not, the simple act of smiling releases feel-good hormones. Next time you're doing your makeup, give yourself a smile. It might feel silly, but it's amazing how a little positivity can change your mood (and your look!).

Breaking Beauty Stereotypes

Beauty comes in all forms, and it's time to let go of unrealistic standards. Here's to the quirky, unique, and authentic – because perfection is overrated!

Embrace Your Features:
If you have freckles, celebrate them! Natural beauty quirks are what make us special. A touch of tinted moisturizer can give you a glow while letting your unique features shine.

Natural Textures Are Beautiful:
Straight, curly, wavy, frizzy – every hair texture has its own beauty. Don't feel pressured to change it up. Instead, try products that enhance your natural texture and let your hair do its thing.

Be Bold:
Whether it's bright lipstick or no makeup at all, the only beauty "rule" is to do what feels good for you. Don't let trends dictate your style. Experiment, play, and most importantly, have fun with it!

Laughing at Beauty Blunders

We've all been there – a new beauty trick gone wrong, a bold look that backfired, or a makeup mishap that just made us laugh. Here are a few relatable, funny stories that prove beauty is more about the fun than the flawless.

The Foundation Face-Off:

One woman shared how she forgot to blend her foundation into her neck before leaving the house. Later that day, she looked in a mirror only to find she'd been walking around with a visible makeup "mask line" the entire time. Lesson learned – double-check in natural light!

The Eyebrow Mishap:

In a moment of inspiration, a young beauty enthusiast decided to fill in her brows a little darker. Let's just say she went from "barely there" to "I'm ready to join a rock band." Her friends couldn't stop laughing, and neither could she.

The Lipstick Teeth Trick:

Trying to pull off a bold red lip? Beware of the lipstick-on-teeth fiasco. One person shared how she was happily chatting away at a party, only to discover that her pearly whites had turned red as well. She had to laugh it off and let it go – after all, beauty mishaps happen to everyone!

The Mascara Disaster:

Ever sneezed right after putting on mascara? It's the ultimate beauty fail, and it's more common than you think! Raccoon eyes, anyone?

In the end, beauty is about feeling comfortable, confident, and uniquely yourself. Whether you're trying a new beauty hack, pampering yourself with a mini spa moment, or laughing at a makeup blunder, remember: beauty isn't about being flawless – it's about enjoying the journey and embracing what makes you, you.

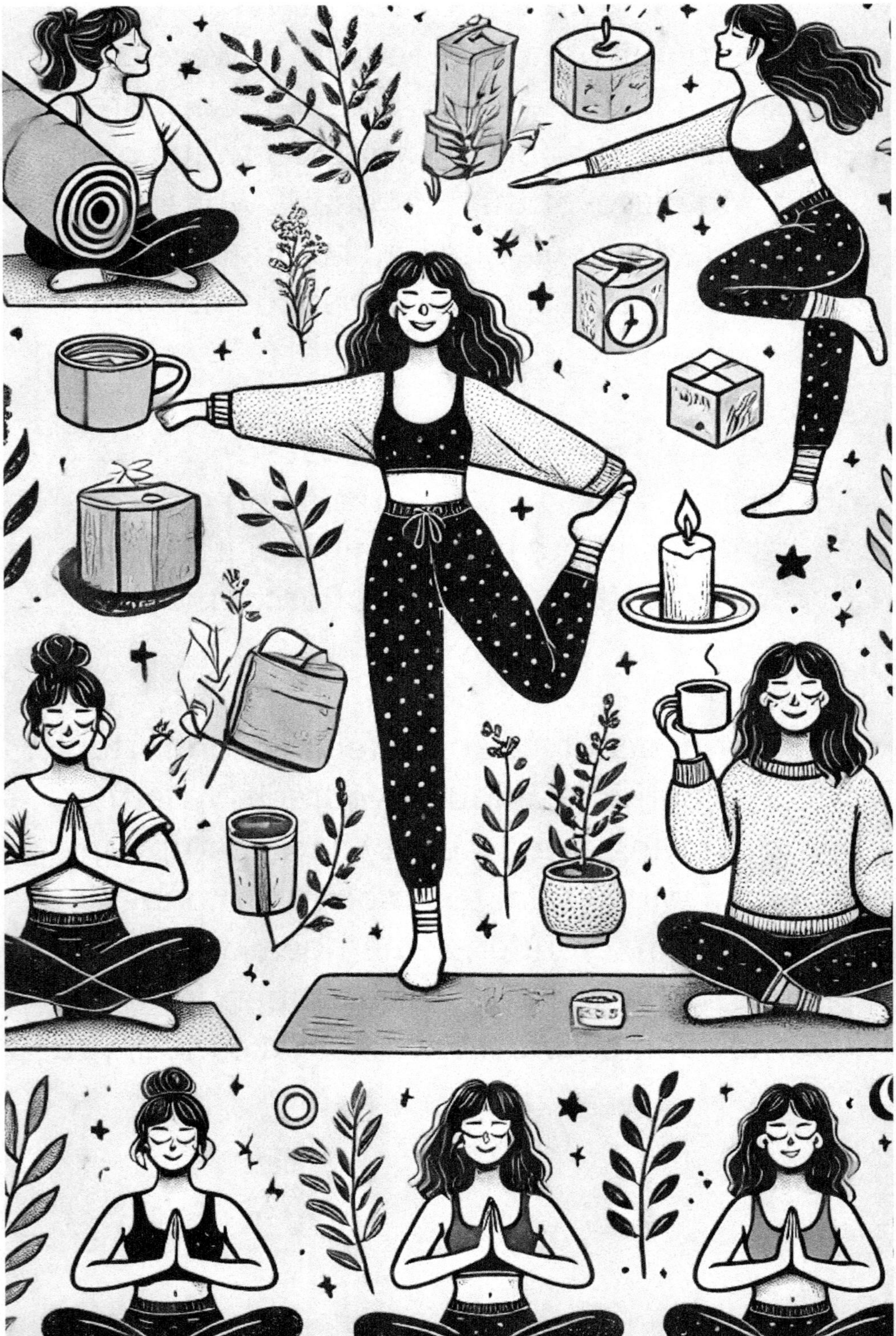

Chapter 3: Wellness Tips for the Busy (and Funny) Woman

Finding time to care for yourself amidst a packed schedule can feel impossible. But wellness isn't about hours spent at a spa or following strict routines; it's about weaving small, simple moments of relaxation, positivity, and humor into your day. This chapter shares wellness tips designed for real life – easy, effective, and just a little bit fun.

1. The Two-Minute Morning Stretch

The morning rush is real, but taking just two minutes to stretch can make a world of difference. Start by stretching your arms overhead, rolling your shoulders, and reaching for the sky. Even if you're still in your pajamas, this mini-stretch session wakes up your muscles and prepares your body for the day ahead.

Add a twist:
Try out a "cat stretch" like your pet might – stretch your back, then give yourself a good shake. Not only does it loosen you up, but it also brings a little humor to the morning routine!

2. Breathe Easy:
Simple Breath Work Anywhere

You don't need a meditation app or even a quiet space to practice deep breathing. The "4-7-8" breathing technique can work wonders to calm you down anywhere – in traffic, at your desk, or even during a hectic grocery run.

Here's how to do it:
- Inhale quietly through your nose for 4 seconds.
- Hold your breath for 7 seconds.
- Exhale slowly through your mouth for 8 seconds.

Repeat this cycle 3–5 times and feel your mind instantly calm down. This trick works wonders for relieving stress and only takes about a minute!

3. The Laugh Break: Wellness for the Soul

Laughter is an underrated wellness tool. The next time you feel overwhelmed, take a short laugh break. Pull up a funny video, read a joke, or simply recall a silly moment from the past. Even forcing a laugh can eventually lead to a genuine chuckle.

Fun fact: Studies show that laughter increases blood flow, which improves heart health and boosts mood. So go ahead, laugh at that cheesy meme – it's officially good for you!

4. Hydration with a Twist: Infuse Your Water

We all know drinking water is essential, but plain water can get, well, plain. Try adding some flavor to your hydration with fruit-infused water. Slice up lemon, cucumber, or strawberries and toss them in your water bottle. Not only does this make drinking water more enjoyable, but it also adds a dose of vitamins.

Pro tip: Make a big batch and keep it in the fridge so it's ready to go when you need a refreshment. And for an added laugh, give each flavor combination a quirky name, like "Berry Blast" or "Cucumber Chill."

5. Dance It Out

We often think of exercise as a chore, but it doesn't have to be. Next time you're feeling sluggish, crank up a favorite song and dance around your living room or kitchen. Dancing is an excellent way to get moving, boost endorphins, and lift your spirits.

Even if it's just a one-minute boogie, you'll feel refreshed. Plus, no one's watching, so go ahead – get as silly as you want.
No judgment, only joy!

6. The Power of "Thank You"

Gratitude is a simple but powerful wellness practice. Take a few seconds each day to thank yourself for something you've done, big or small. Maybe you got through a long day, made a great cup of coffee, or simply remembered to call a friend.

Keeping a mini gratitude journal or mentally listing things you're grateful for at bedtime can help shift your mindset, especially on tough days. Before you know it, you'll feel lighter and more appreciative of the small joys in life.

7. Pamper Hands and Feet: Mini Spa Moments

Even the busiest days offer a moment for pampering. Applying lotion to your hands and feet isn't just about moisture – it's a mini massage! Choose a scent you love, and take a minute to gently massage your hands and feet, especially if you've been on the go all day.

Add a little bonus: Pop on cozy socks afterward to lock in the moisture and make it a cozy ritual before bed.

8. Phone-Free Zone: Reclaim Your Time

Screens are everywhere, and while they keep us connected, they can also drain our energy. Choose a small part of your day, even just ten minutes, to go completely phone-free. Use this time to read a book, step outside, or just enjoy a few moments of quiet.

For an extra challenge, make your bedroom a "no-phone zone" after a certain time in the evening. You'd be surprised at how refreshing this small break can be for your mind!

9. Light a Candle, Brighten Your Day

Scents have a powerful effect on our mood, and lighting a candle or using essential oils can change the entire vibe of a space. Scents like lavender and chamomile are known for their calming effects, while citrus and peppermint can uplift your spirits.

Pro tip: Light a candle in your favorite scent when you're winding down for the night, or even during a bubble bath. It's a small act of self-care, but it makes a big difference in creating a peaceful atmosphere.

10. Declutter One Space for Instant Calm

A cluttered space can make us feel overwhelmed, so taking a few minutes to declutter just one area – your desk, nightstand, or even a kitchen drawer – can bring a surprising sense of relief.

Wellness doesn't require hours of time, expensive products, or rigid routines. It's all about small, intentional choices that bring you joy, comfort, and a bit of laughter. So embrace these little moments of self-care, and remember – wellness is a journey, not a destination. Enjoy every step along the way!

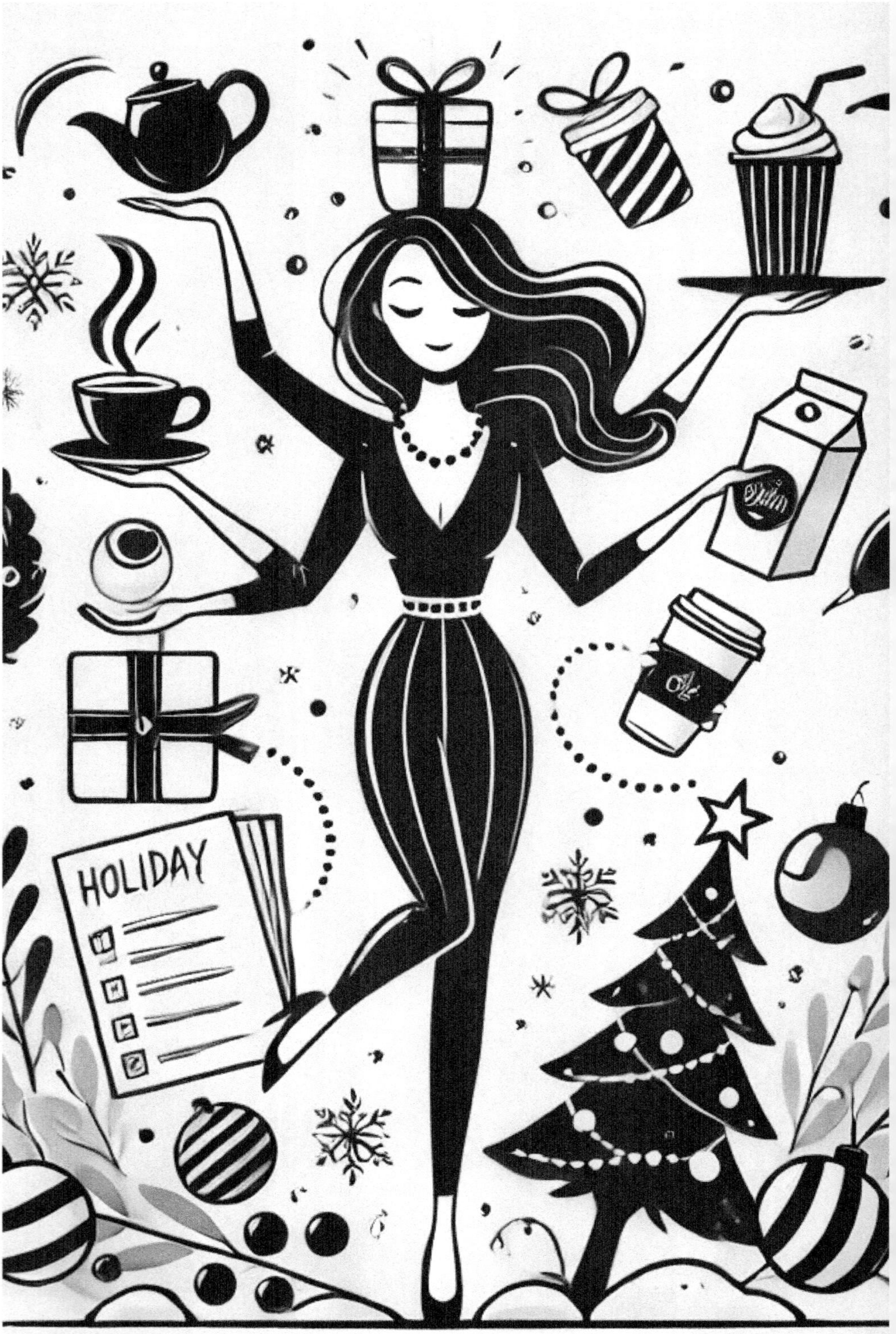
HOLIDAY

Chapter 4: Everyday Dilemmas
(and How to Deal with Them)

Life's little challenges have a way of sneaking up on us, from decision-making dilemmas to everyday mishaps that can leave us scratching our heads or laughing out loud. This chapter is all about embracing these moments with humor, grace, and a few tips to make navigating them a little easier. We'll explore simple solutions, quick mental resets, and reminders that even the most organized among us aren't immune to daily hiccups.

1. The "What to Wear" Struggle

We've all been there: staring into the closet, feeling as if we have nothing to wear. Somehow, even with racks full of options, the right outfit can feel elusive. Here's how to make dressing simpler and more fun.

Plan Around One Piece:
Start with one item you feel like wearing – maybe it's a cozy sweater or your favorite jeans. Build the rest of your outfit around it, rather than trying to put together a perfect ensemble from scratch.

Create a Uniform:
For days when decision fatigue hits, have a go-to "uniform." It could be jeans, a nice top, and ankle boots, or a dress with sneakers. Having a go-to combo saves you the mental energy and always looks good.

Organize by Occasion:
Divide your closet into categories like workwear, casual, or going out. When you need something specific, you know exactly where to go, and you'll spend less time in a fashion crisis.

2. The Battle with Procrastination

Procrastination affects us all. Somehow, tasks can always wait a little longer, whether it's doing laundry, organizing your workspace, or finally tackling that email inbox. Here's how to tackle procrastination without feeling overwhelmed.

The 5-Minute Rule:
If a task takes less than five minutes, do it immediately. This rule helps avoid tasks piling up, and you'll often find that once you start, you'll want to keep going.

Set a Timer:
For bigger tasks, set a timer for 10–15 minutes and work on the task during that time. Knowing there's an endpoint can make it easier to get started, and once the timer goes off, you may feel motivated to keep going.

Reward Yourself:
Give yourself a small reward for completing a task you've been putting off. Even something as simple as a cup of coffee or a 10-minute break can make getting things done more appealing.

3. Decision Fatigue:
When Even Simple Choices Feel Hard

From picking a restaurant to deciding what to watch, decision fatigue is real, especially when life is already full of choices. These tips help streamline decision-making for easier, faster choices.

Limit Options:
Rather than scrolling endlessly through options, limit yourself to a few top choices. When picking a restaurant, narrow it down to two or three places and decide based on what you feel like most in the moment.

Pre-Made Decisions:
For recurring choices, like what to eat for lunch, have a set of pre-made options that you can choose from quickly. Pre-made decisions save time and help prevent feeling drained by too many daily choices.

Flip a Coin:
If you're still stuck, flip a coin. Sometimes, a coin toss helps reveal what you actually want, based on your reaction to the result.

4. The Search for Lost Items

Who hasn't lost their keys, phone, or sunglasses when they're running out the door? The good news is there are ways to minimize the frustration of losing things.

Create a Landing Zone:
Designate a spot near your front door for essentials like keys, wallet, and sunglasses. A "landing zone" keeps everything in one place, making it easier to grab and go.

Use a Tracking Device:
Consider using a small tracking device for items that tend to wander, like keys or your phone. Many devices pair with your phone, so you can quickly locate missing items without stress.

The 10-Second Memory Trick:
When you put something down, take 10 seconds to note where it is. This simple mental check-in can help reinforce memory and make items easier to find later.

5. The Mystery of the Unread Notifications

The constant buzz of notifications can feel overwhelming, but it can also create a strange sense of guilt – those unread messages and emails just sitting there, waiting. Here's how to keep it under control without drowning in notifications.

Daily Declutter:
Set a daily time (maybe once in the morning, once at night) to check and clear notifications. Limiting it to specific times prevents the feeling of being "on call" all day.

Prioritize the Important Ones:
Filter your notifications so only the most essential ones pop up. Group less critical ones (like app updates) together so they don't interrupt you throughout the day.

The Rule of Two:
Try to keep your unread notifications to two or fewer. This helps you stay on top of things without letting messages pile up, making it easier to tackle them gradually.

6. Cooking Chaos: Dinner Dilemmas

Not everyone is a natural-born chef, and deciding what to cook (or where to order from) can feel like a daily dilemma. Here's how to simplify meal planning without losing your sanity.

The "One-Pot Wonder" Solution:

On busy nights, opt for a one-pot meal. Whether it's pasta, a stir-fry, or soup, one-pot meals save time on cooking and cleanup.

Plan a Weekly Menu:

Take a few minutes at the start of the week to plan your meals. This doesn't mean cooking in advance – just decide what's on the menu. It eliminates daily decision-making and helps you stay organized with groceries.

Frozen Essentials:

Keep a few go-to frozen items on hand, like veggies, pre-cooked rice, or frozen protein options. It makes putting together a last-minute meal easy when you don't have fresh ingredients.

7. Budget Balancing

Managing finances is one of life's biggest and most constant challenges. Here's how to stay on top of budgeting in a way that's stress-free and manageable.

The 50/30/20 Rule:
This rule divides your income into three categories: 50% for essentials (like rent and groceries), 30% for discretionary spending, and 20% for savings. It's an easy guideline to follow without having to track every dollar.

Automate Your Savings:
Set up automatic transfers to your savings account each month. Even small amounts add up, and you'll be building your savings without thinking about it.

Track Just a Few Big Items:
If tracking every little expense feels overwhelming, focus on a few key categories, like dining out or shopping. This gives you a clear picture of where your money is going without needing to monitor every detail.

8. Finding Time to Relax

Sometimes, relaxing can feel like a chore when life is constantly busy. Here's how to carve out small moments of relaxation in your day.

Set a Non-Negotiable Break:

Make it a rule to take a 10-minute break each afternoon. Use it to grab a coffee, step outside, or just stretch. These small, non-negotiable breaks can refresh you without requiring major time commitments.

Mindful Moments:

Take a few seconds throughout the day to practice mindfulness – like paying attention to your breath or focusing on a specific sound. Even a few mindful moments can help you reset and stay focused.

Everyday dilemmas may be small, but they're also the fabric of daily life. Embracing them with humor and a sense of calm makes all the difference. Whether it's picking an outfit, finding time to relax, or keeping track of your budget, remember: there's no perfect solution, but small changes add up to a smoother, happier day.

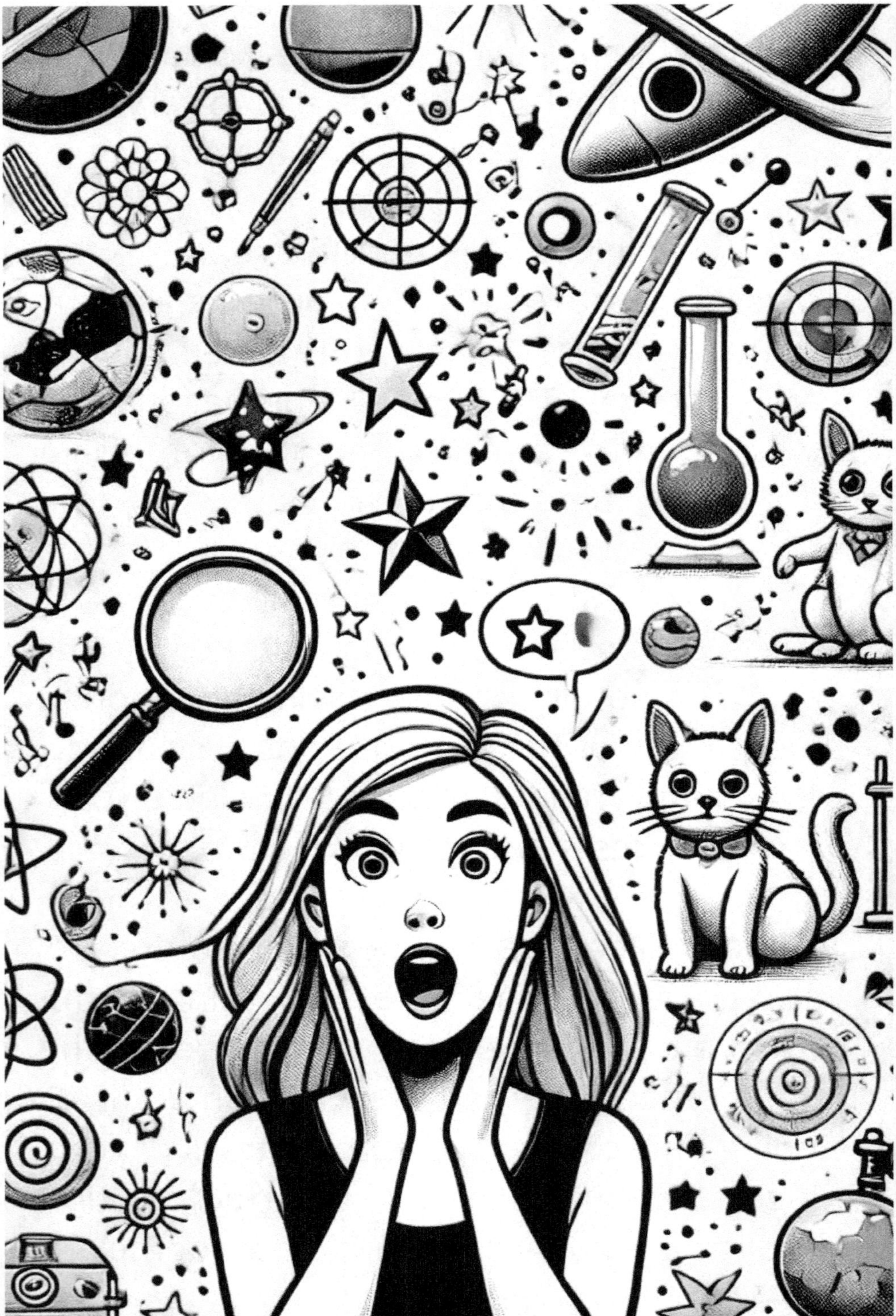

Chapter 5: Fun Facts to Amaze and Amuse

We all love a good fun fact – those little nuggets of information that surprise us, make us laugh, or teach us something new. In this chapter, we dive into some of the most amusing, strange, and downright fascinating facts from around the world. From curious tidbits about animals and history to quirky discoveries in science and food, these fun facts are here to entertain and maybe even make you the star of your next trivia night!

1. Animal Antics: Surprising Facts About Our Furry (and Not-So-Furry) Friends

Cows Have Best Friends: Studies show that cows form strong bonds with specific other cows and can become stressed when separated from their best buddies.

Dolphins Call Each Other by Name:
Dolphins have a unique way of identifying each other – each dolphin develops its own "whistle," almost like a name, and the others recognize and use that whistle to communicate.

Octopuses Have Three Hearts:
That's right – octopuses have not one, not two, but three hearts! Two pump blood to their gills, while the third pumps it to the rest of the body. Fun fact: when an octopus swims, the heart pumping blood to its body actually stops.

Rats Laugh When Tickled:
Yes, it's true – when you tickle a rat, it produces high-pitched "giggles" that are undetectable to the human ear but can be heard with special equipment.

Pigeons Can Do Math:
Believe it or not, pigeons have been shown to be able to understand abstract mathematical concepts. In some studies, pigeons have even demonstrated the ability to count and organize items by number.

2. Weird History: Strange Stories from the Past

Napoleon Was Once Attacked by Bunnies: In a strange historical event, Napoleon Bonaparte once ordered a rabbit hunt, but the plan backfired. When the rabbits were released, they charged at Napoleon instead of running away, forcing him to flee.

Cleopatra Wasn't Egyptian: While Cleopatra is often associated with ancient Egypt, she was actually of Macedonian-Greek descent. As a member of the Ptolemaic dynasty, her family ruled Egypt after Alexander the Great's conquest.

George Washington Was a Whiskey Tycoon: Founding Father George Washington was not only the first U.S. President but also one of the country's most successful whiskey distillers. His distillery at Mount Vernon was the largest in America at the time.

Shakespeare Invented Over 1,700 Words: The famous playwright William Shakespeare is credited with creating over 1,700 words we still use today, including "fashionable," "swagger," and "lonely."

3. Science Mysteries

Bananas Are Berries, But Strawberries Aren't:
In botanical terms, bananas are actually classified as berries, while strawberries are not. True berries have seeds inside them, which bananas do, but strawberries don't.

Water Can Boil and Freeze at the Same Time:
In a scientific phenomenon called the "triple point," water can exist in solid, liquid, and gas forms simultaneously if the temperature and pressure are just right.

The Eiffel Tower Grows in Summer:
Due to thermal expansion, the Eiffel Tower can grow up to 6 inches taller in the summer heat. When temperatures drop, it shrinks back to its original height.

Hot Water Freezes Faster Than Cold:
Known as the Mpemba effect, hot water can actually freeze faster than cold water in certain conditions, though scientists are still trying to fully understand why.

Some Clouds Weigh Over a Million Pounds:
The fluffy white clouds we see can weigh as much as a million pounds. They appear light because the weight is spread across a massive area.

4. Foodie Facts: Bizarre and Fun Facts About Food

Honey Never Spoils:

Honey is the only food that never expires. Archaeologists have found pots of honey in ancient Egyptian tombs that are over 3,000 years old and still edible.

Peanuts Aren't Nuts:

Despite their name, peanuts aren't nuts at all – they're legumes, like beans and lentils. True nuts grow on trees, while peanuts grow underground.

Carrots Used to Be Purple:

Carrots were originally purple, not orange. It wasn't until the 17th century that Dutch farmers began cultivating orange carrots in honor of the royal House of Orange.

Chocolate Was Once Used as Currency:

In ancient Mesoamerica, the Aztecs used cacao beans as currency. They prized chocolate so highly that they traded it just like money.

Pineapples Take Two Years to Grow:

Pineapples are one of the slowest-growing fruits, taking up to two years to mature. This is why they're often considered a tropical luxury!

5. Human Body Wonders: Incredible Things About Ourselves

We're Taller in the Morning: Believe it or not, you're slightly taller in the morning than at night. Throughout the day, gravity compresses the cartilage in your spine, making you a tiny bit shorter by bedtime.

Your Stomach Gets a New Lining Every 3-4 Days: The stomach's acidic environment is so harsh that it constantly needs to renew its lining to avoid digesting itself!

You Can't Breathe and Swallow at the Same Time: This is because the same part of our throat is used for both breathing and swallowing, making it impossible to do both simultaneously.

You Shed About 40 Pounds of Skin in a Lifetime: The average human sheds around 40 pounds of skin cells over their lifetime. Most of the dust you see around is actually composed of dead skin cells!

6. Odd Laws from Around the World

It's Illegal to Chew Gum in Singapore: Singapore has strict laws about cleanliness, and chewing gum is actually banned to keep public spaces clean. Only medicinal gum is allowed, and you need a prescription for it.

In Switzerland, You Can't Flush After 10 PM: In some Swiss apartment buildings, it's illegal to flush the toilet after 10 PM, as it's considered noise pollution.

In France, It's Illegal to Name a Pig Napoleon: Out of respect for the historical figure Napoleon Bonaparte, it's illegal in France to name a pig "Napoleon."

In the UK, It's Illegal to Die in Parliament: According to an old law in the UK, it's technically illegal to die in the Houses of Parliament, as doing so would entitle the deceased to a state funeral.

In Samoa, It's Illegal to Forget Your Wife's Birthday: In Samoa, it's illegal for husbands to forget their wife's birthday. Forgetting this special day could result in a fine or worse!

7. Space Oddities: Fascinating Facts About the Universe

A Day on Venus Is Longer Than Its Year: Venus takes longer to rotate on its axis (243 Earth days) than it does to orbit the Sun (225 Earth days), meaning a day on Venus is longer than a year.

There Are More Stars Than Grains of Sand on Earth: Scientists estimate that the observable universe contains more stars than there are grains of sand on all the beaches of Earth.

Neutron Stars Are Incredibly Dense: A teaspoon of matter from a neutron star would weigh about 6 billion tons on Earth. Neutron stars are so dense that they defy imagination.

Space Isn't Actually "Silent": Although there's no atmosphere to carry sound, scientists have detected radio emissions from stars and planets, giving space its own strange "sound."

In a world full of fascinating mysteries and odd facts, there's always something new to learn. We hope these quirky and amusing tidbits inspire you to look at life with curiosity and maybe share some of these facts with friends – after all, who doesn't love a good fun fact?

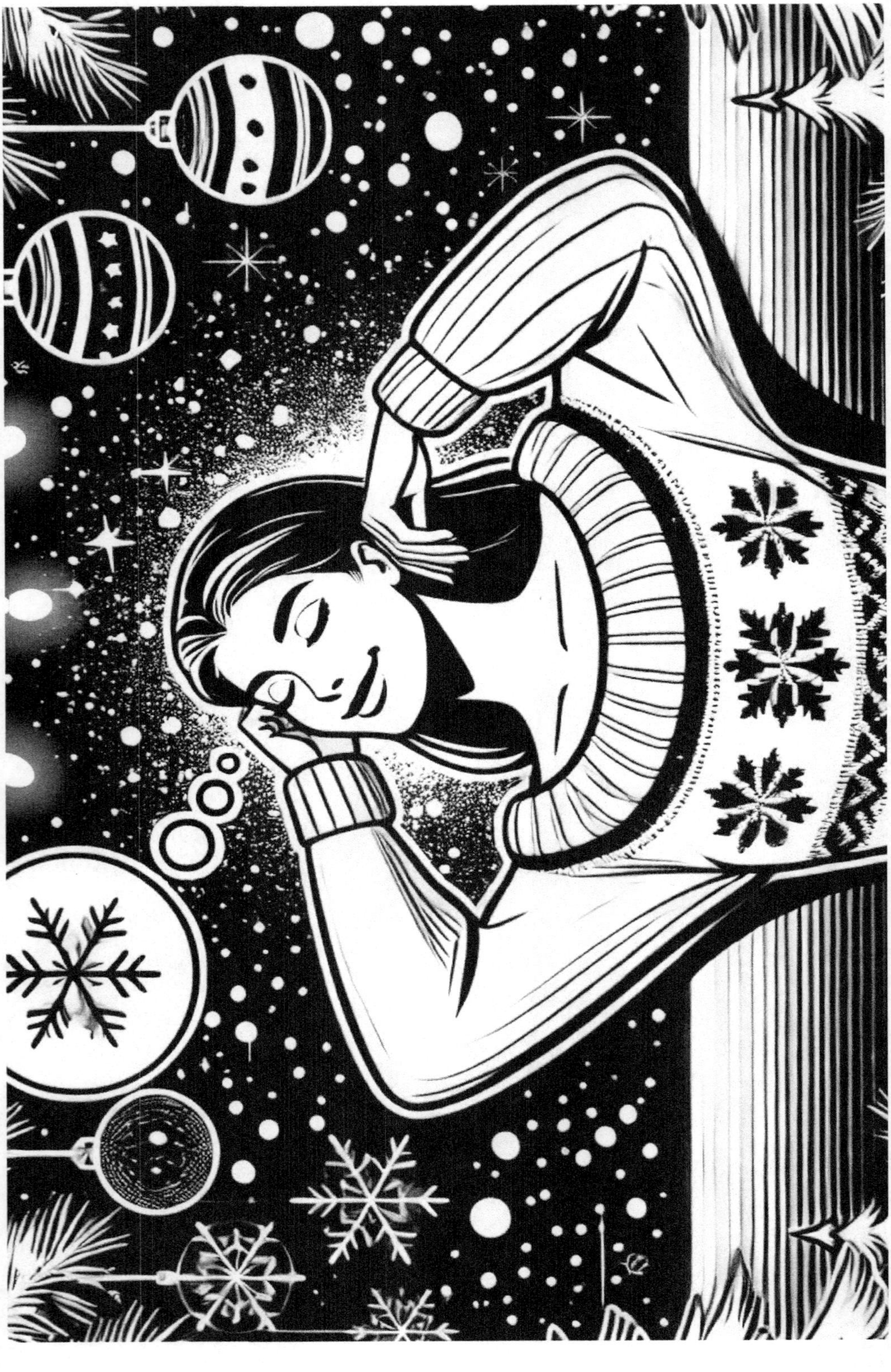

Chapter 6:
Positive Thoughts for a Quick Break

In the hustle and bustle of daily life, sometimes all we need is a quick mental reset – a moment to breathe, refocus, and fill our minds with positive thoughts. This chapter offers a collection of uplifting quotes, mini-reflections, and easy exercises to boost your mood, even on the busiest of days. Each one is designed to remind you of the simple joys, encourage mindfulness, and help you find little pockets of peace.

1. Morning Mantras: Start Your Day Right

Starting your day with a positive mindset can make a huge difference. These morning mantras are short and powerful, easy to repeat while brushing your teeth or sipping your first cup of coffee.

"Today is a new day, filled with endless possibilities."
– This reminder can shift your focus from any worries or stresses and open your mind to the good things the day can bring.

"I am capable, calm, and in control."
– Great for days when you're feeling overwhelmed, this mantra centers you and helps create a sense of calm.

"I choose to focus on what I can control."
– When things feel chaotic, this saying can help you put your energy into what's within your reach, letting go of what you can't change.

2. Quick Gratitude Check-In

Taking a few moments to feel gratitude can change your entire outlook on the day. Here's a quick and simple exercise to practice anytime.

Name Three Things You're Grateful For Right Now:

They can be big or small – your health, a favorite song, a warm cup of tea, or a recent compliment. Let yourself feel genuine appreciation for each one.

Write Down One Positive Thing that Happened Today:

Even if it was a simple moment, writing it down solidifies it in your memory, allowing you to focus on the good and reframe your day.

Thank Someone (Even if Only in Your Mind):

Think of someone who has recently helped or inspired you, and mentally thank them. It doesn't have to be big; even small gestures are worth appreciation. Practicing gratitude towards others builds positive emotions.

3. "In the Moment" Breathing Exercise

Breathing exercises can be practiced anywhere – at your desk, in line at the grocery store, or even in traffic. Here's a quick one that helps reduce stress and refocus your thoughts.

Box Breathing:
Visualize drawing a box as you breathe. Inhale for 4 counts, hold for 4 counts, exhale for 4 counts, and pause for 4 counts. Repeat this cycle a few times. It's calming, centers you, and takes less than a minute.

The 5-5-5 Technique:
Inhale deeply for 5 seconds, hold for 5 seconds, and then exhale slowly for 5 seconds. Repeat until you feel calm. This simple exercise helps quiet the mind and recharge.

4. The Power of a Smile

Smiling, even when you're not feeling it, can actually lift your mood. This small action releases endorphins, reduces stress, and can even make you feel more confident.

Fake It 'Til You Feel It:
Smiling, even if it feels forced at first, can actually lead to genuine feelings of happiness. Try it next time you're feeling down – just a few seconds can make a difference.

Smile at Someone You Don't Know:
Whether it's a passerby, the barista at your coffee shop, or a coworker in the hallway, exchanging smiles can create a mini moment of connection that leaves you both feeling good.

Mirror Smile:
Stand in front of the mirror, look yourself in the eyes, and give yourself a smile. It might feel silly, but it's a fun way to remind yourself that you're worth a little kindness.

5. Short Uplifting Quotes for Any Moment

Sometimes a single phrase can turn your whole day around. These short, uplifting quotes are perfect for those times when you need a quick boost.

"Happiness is not by chance, but by choice." – Jim Rohn

"Be the reason someone smiles today."

"You don't have to control your thoughts. You just have to stop letting them control you." – Dan Millman

"One small positive thought can change your whole day." – Zig Ziglar

"Wherever you are, be all there." – Jim Elliot

Feel free to pick a favorite and use it as a personal mantra. Write it down somewhere you'll see it throughout the day, like your desk, planner, or phone screen.

6. The "Tiny Wins" Mindset

Celebrating small achievements is a great way to keep yourself motivated. Tiny wins may seem insignificant, but they add up and can bring a sense of accomplishment and pride.

List Today's Tiny Wins:
It could be as simple as drinking enough water, getting through a challenging task, or making your bed. Recognize each little win and let yourself feel proud – you're accomplishing more than you think!

Turn "I Have to" into "I Get to":
Reframing your to-do list can turn mundane tasks into moments of gratitude. Instead of "I have to do the dishes," try "I get to do the dishes because I have food to eat."

Create a Tiny Win Ritual:
At the end of each day, jot down one small accomplishment. Over time, this will become a habit that helps you focus on the positive, building confidence in yourself and your abilities.

7. Quick Kindness Challenge

Practicing small acts of kindness can boost your mood, improve your relationships, and even make you feel healthier. These mini challenges are easy, fun, and rewarding.

Send a Compliment:

Message or call someone to share a compliment or acknowledge something you appreciate about them. It's a quick act that can make their day – and yours.

Leave a Note of Encouragement:

Leave a sticky note with an uplifting message in a random place, like on a mirror, your fridge, or even in a library book. Imagine the smile it could bring to someone who finds it.

Give Yourself a Pep Talk:

Sometimes, the person who needs kindness most is you. Take a moment to give yourself a mental pep talk. Remind yourself of a recent accomplishment or simply tell yourself that you're doing great!

8. Visualize Your Happy Place

When stress kicks in, take a mental vacation to your happy place. Visualization is a powerful tool that allows you to mentally "travel" to a place of peace and joy, even if you can't physically be there.

Close Your Eyes and Imagine:
Think of a place that brings you peace – maybe it's a beach, a quiet forest, or a cozy room. Visualize every detail: the colors, sounds, smells, and textures.

Feel the Calm:
As you picture yourself there, let your body relax and imagine the peace of being in that space. Even a 30-second escape can bring you back feeling refreshed.

Combine with Deep Breathing:
Deep breathing while visualizing helps to deepen the relaxation. Inhale slowly, imagine yourself surrounded by calm, then exhale all stress.

9. End the Day with Reflection

Ending your day with positive thoughts can help you sleep better and wake up feeling more refreshed. Here are some simple end-of-day reflections to try.

What's One Good Thing About Today?:
No matter how the day went, find at least one good thing that happened. It could be as simple as enjoying a good meal or having a few minutes to relax.

Something I Learned Today:
Reflecting on one new thing you learned or experienced helps bring a sense of growth and curiosity to each day, no matter how small.

What Am I Looking Forward to Tomorrow?:
Ending the day with something to look forward to can boost your mood and help you feel more excited for tomorrow. Even small things – like a morning coffee or reading a new chapter in a book – can make a difference.

Amid daily demands, a quick reset – like a mantra, gratitude, or a mental escape – builds a foundation of calm for each day.

Chapter 7:
Just for Laughs – Quizzes and Mini-Tests

Sometimes, all we need is a quick laugh or a lighthearted escape from the daily grind. In this chapter, you'll find a collection of fun, quirky quizzes and mini-tests that are designed to entertain and bring out your playful side. From discovering your "spirit snack" to testing your "laugh style," these activities are here to brighten your day, bring a smile to your face, and maybe even reveal something funny about yourself!

1. What's Your Spirit Snack?

Everyone has a snack that embodies their personality. Find out which treat matches your vibe with this quick quiz!

It's a lazy Sunday afternoon – what's your ideal activity?

A) Watching your favorite show in pajamas
B) Going for a walk in the park
C) Baking something delicious
D) Trying out a new hobby or DIY project

How would your friends describe you?
A) Laid-back and chill
B) Sweet and supportive
C) Creative and adventurous
D) Fun-loving and energetic

Pick a flavor that speaks to you.
A) Salty B) Sweet C) Savory D) Spicy

What's your favorite way to unwind after a long day?
A) A bubble bath
B) Cuddling with a pet or loved one
C) Cooking or crafting
D) Dancing to your favorite music

Results:

Mostly A's – **You're a Potato Chip!** Laid-back and easygoing, you're the perfect comfort food friend.

Mostly B's – You're a **Chocolate Chip Cookie!** Sweet and dependable, everyone loves having you around.

Mostly C's – **You're a Cheese Board!** Unique and a bit fancy, you bring flavor and creativity to any gathering.

Mostly D's – **You're a Spicy Popcorn!** Fun and full of energy, you're always up for something new and exciting.

2. What's Your Laugh Style?

Do you have a contagious giggle, a silent shake, or maybe even a full-on snort? Find out your unique laugh style here!

When you watch a funny movie, your laugh is:
A) A light chuckle
B) A loud belly laugh
C) A silent, shaking giggle
D) A mix of giggles and snorts

Your friends are most likely to describe your laugh as:
A) Quiet but contagious
B) Bold and booming
C) Silent but hilarious
D) Unexpected and silly

When you find something REALLY funny, you:
A) Try to hold it in (and end up laughing even more)
B) Let it out – loud and proud!
C) Double over, unable to make a sound
D) Start laughing and can't stop, adding sound effects as you go

Results:

Mostly A's – **You're a Gentle Giggle**! Quiet but endearing, your laugh adds warmth to any situation.

Mostly B's – **You're a Belly Laugher!** Your laugh is loud and proud, and it makes others laugh even more.

Mostly C's – **You're a Silent Shaker!** Even without sound, your laugh is unmistakable, and your body language says it all.

Mostly D's – **You're a Snorty Chuckler!** Your laugh is quirky and unique, and it always catches others by surprise.

3. Which Famous Meme Are You?

Memes add humor to our lives, and if you were one, what would you be? Take this quiz to find out which famous meme you embody!

How do you react to unexpected news?
A) Shrug it off and go with the flow
B) Laugh uncontrollably
C) Make a sarcastic comment
D) Take a dramatic gasp

Your ideal weekend plan involves:
A) Catching up on sleep
B) Going out with friends
C) People-watching and making jokes
D) Trying something new and exciting

Your friends would describe your sense of humor as:
A) Chill and unbothered
B) Silly and over-the-top
C) Dry and witty
D) Dramatic and expressive

Results:

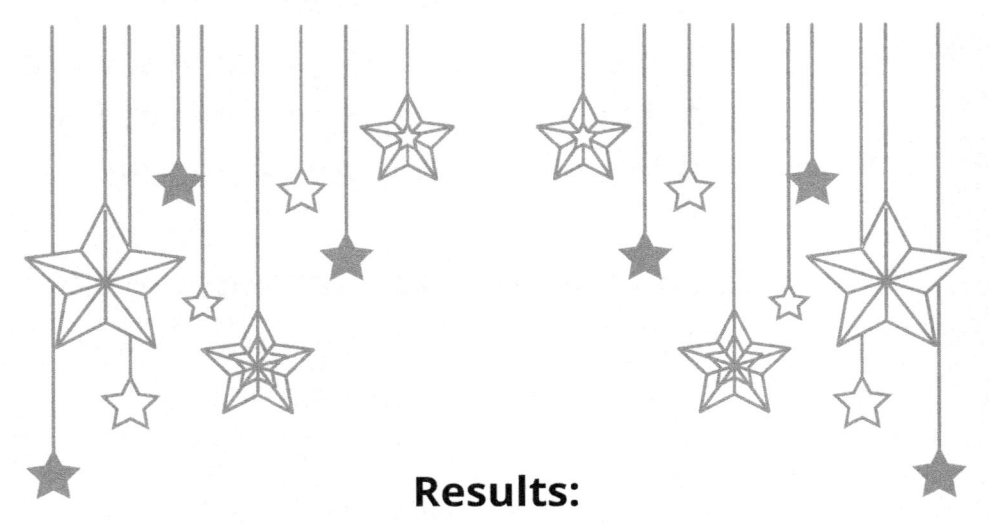

Mostly A's – You're the **"This is Fine"** Meme! Chill in the face of chaos, you go with the flow, no matter what.

Mostly B's – You're the **"LOL Cat"** Meme! Playful and lighthearted, you bring joy to everyone around you.

Mostly C's – You're the **"Grumpy Cat"** Meme! With a dash of sarcasm and a dry sense of humor, you're always ready with a clever remark.

Mostly D's – You're the **"Dramatic Chipmunk"** Meme! Expressive and a bit theatrical, you keep everyone entertained with your reactions.

4. What's Your Ideal Pet Companion?

Pets have personalities too! If you could have any animal as a loyal companion, which one would be your perfect match? Find out here!

Your ideal day involves:
A) Chilling on the couch
B) Going on a short, leisurely walk
C) Exploring new places
D) Lots of activity and excitement

Which best describes you?
A) Calm and laid-back
B) Loyal and caring
C) Adventurous and curious
D) Playful and energetic

You prefer animals that are:
A) Low-maintenance and independent
B) Cuddly and affectionate
C) Adventurous and smart
D) Fun-loving and active

Results:

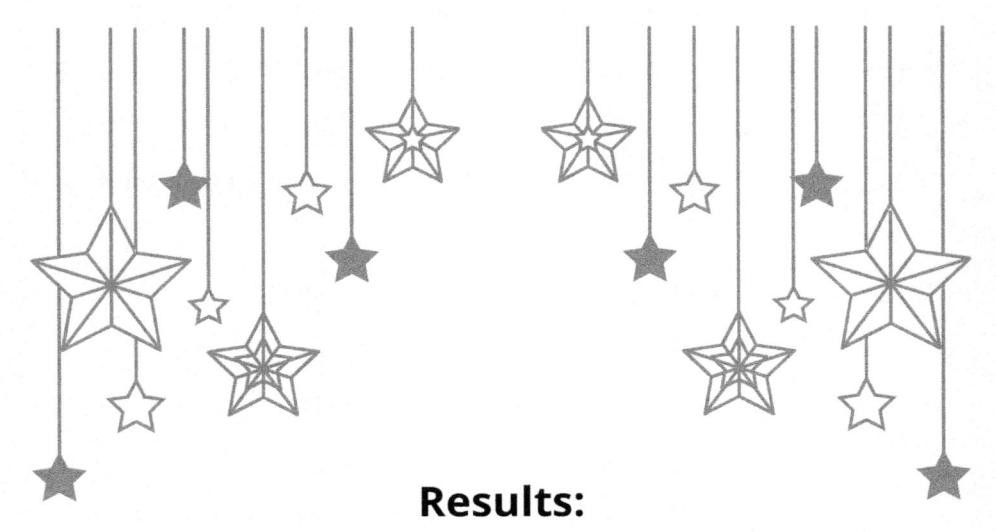

Mostly A's – **You're a Cat Person!** Independent and relaxed, you appreciate a companion who's equally laid-back.

Mostly B's – **You're a Dog Lover!** Loyal and friendly, you'd love a pet who's always there to greet you with a wagging tail.

Mostly C's – **You're a Parrot Pal!** Curious and adventurous, you need a companion as inquisitive as you are.

Mostly D's – **You're a Hamster Buddy!** Full of energy and enthusiasm, a playful pet would be your perfect match.

5. What's Your Superpower?

Ever wondered what superpower best matches your personality?
Take this mini-test to find out!

How do you handle challenges?
A) Think it through and stay calm
B) Rely on your instincts
C) Find the humor in the situation
D) Tackle it head-on with energy

Friends rely on you for:
A) Thoughtful advice
B) Support and empathy
C) Laughter and positivity
D) Getting things done

What's your strongest quality?
A) Patience
B) Kindness
C) Sense of humor
D) Determination

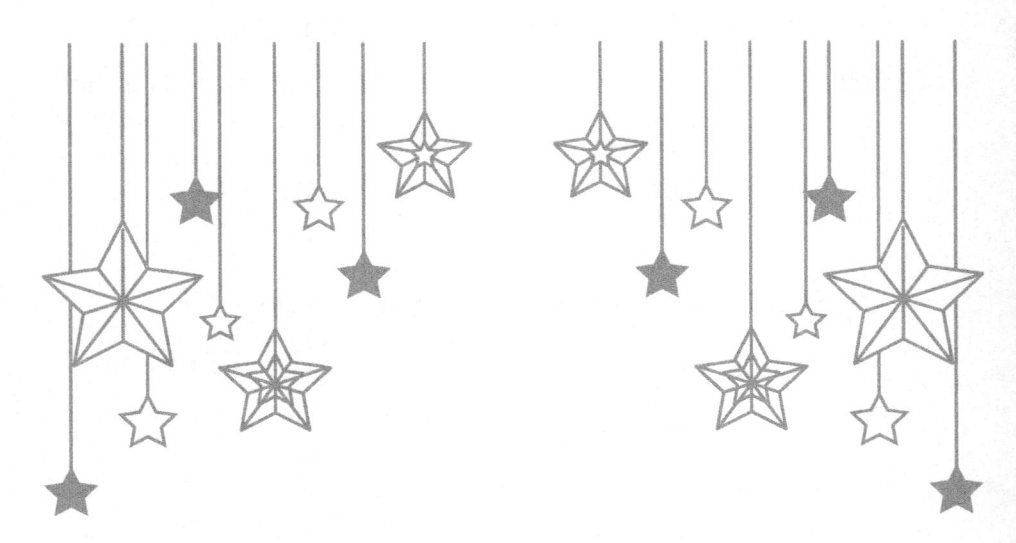

Results:

Mostly A's – **Mind Reader!** You're a calm observer who picks up on what others are thinking and feeling.

Mostly B's – **Empathy Power!** You understand people deeply and can sense what they need most.

Mostly C's – **Laughter Vibes!** You brighten any room with your humor and make even the hardest days lighter.

Mostly D's – **Energy Burst!** Determined and unstoppable, you power through anything that comes your way.

6. Where's Your Dream Destination?
Where would your dream vacation take you? Find out which destination matches your travel style!

Your ideal vacation is:
A) Relaxing by the water
B) Exploring local culture
C) Trying exciting outdoor activities
D) Wandering through a bustling city

What sounds most exciting?
A) A beach resort
B) A charming village
C) A mountain lodge
D) A city with vibrant nightlife

Your travel goal is to:
A) Unwind and recharge
B) Immerse yourself in culture
C) Experience adventure
D) Enjoy the hustle and bustle

Results:

Mostly A's – **You belong on a Tropical Island!** Relaxing and laid-back, you're all about beach vibes and sunshine.

Mostly B's – **You'd love a European Countryside Escape!** Full of charm and culture, you're drawn to cozy villages and quiet towns.

Mostly C's – **The Rocky Mountains are calling!** Adventurous and energetic, you thrive on outdoor challenges.

Mostly D's – **You're a City Explorer!** Vibrant and social, you find excitement in the fast pace and energy of city life.

Whether you're discovering your spirit snack or figuring out your dream destination, these quizzes are a lighthearted way to take a break and learn a little more about yourself. Enjoy the laughs, share your results with friends, and remember – sometimes, the best moments come from simply being playful and having fun!

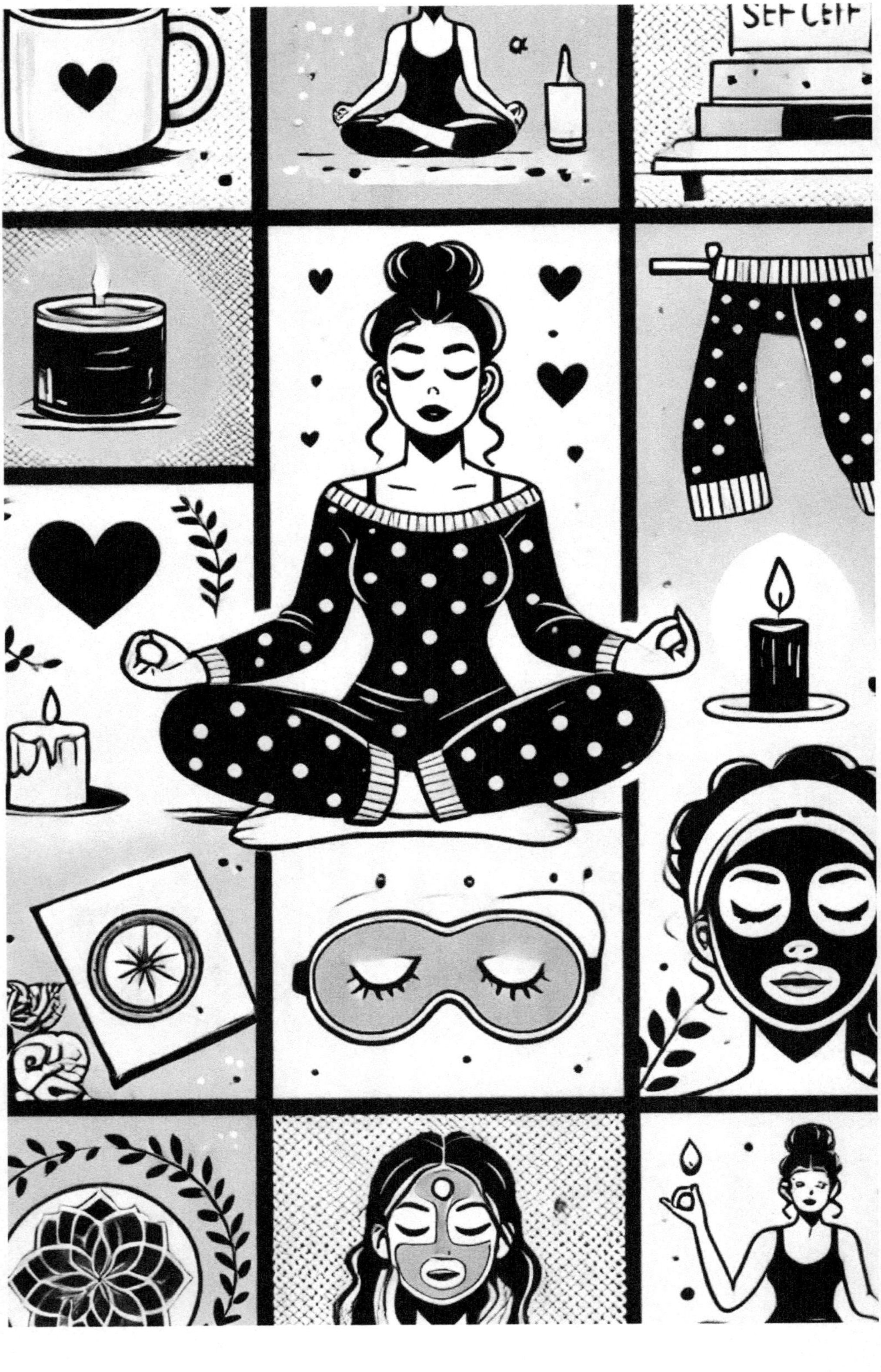
SEF CEIF

Chapter 8: Self-Care Ideas for Every Mood

Self-care isn't one-size-fits-all; it depends on how you're feeling at any given moment. Whether you're feeling stressed, tired, or just in need of a little extra TLC, this chapter offers a variety of self-care ideas that match different moods. From relaxing rituals to energizing activities, here's how to take care of yourself no matter what kind of day you're having.

1. When You're Feeling Stressed: Calm and Recenter

Stress can make everything feel overwhelming, but taking a few moments to focus on yourself can make a huge difference. Here are some calming self-care activities to help you destress and find your center.

Practice Deep Breathing:

Sit in a comfortable position, close your eyes, and take slow, deep breaths. Try inhaling for 4 seconds, holding for 7 seconds, and exhaling for 8 seconds. This helps to calm your nervous system and bring you back to a relaxed state.

Take a Warm Bath:
Add some Epsom salts, essential oils, or even just a few drops of lavender oil to your bath. Soak in the warmth for at least 15 minutes, allowing your muscles to relax and your mind to unwind.

Listen to Calming Music or Nature Sounds:
Find a playlist of peaceful music or nature sounds like ocean waves or birds chirping. Sit back, close your eyes, and let the soothing sounds wash away your stress.

Journal It Out:
Sometimes, writing down your worries can help relieve stress. Grab a journal and let yourself write freely. It doesn't have to be structured; just let your thoughts flow onto the page.

2. When You're Feeling Tired: Rest and Recharge

When exhaustion hits, it's essential to slow down and give yourself a chance to recover. These restful self-care ideas will help you restore your energy without pushing yourself too hard.

Take a Power Nap:
A 20-30 minute nap can give you the boost you need to feel more awake and alert. Just set an alarm to avoid oversleeping, which can make you feel groggy.

Try a Soothing Face Mask:
A hydrating face mask can be refreshing and relaxing. Lie down, close your eyes, and let the mask do its work while you rest.

Do a Light Stretching Routine:
Gentle stretches help release muscle tension and get your blood flowing without too much effort. Stretch your arms, shoulders, back, and legs to relieve any stiffness.

Have a Cup of Herbal Tea:
Choose a calming herbal tea like chamomile or peppermint. The warmth and soothing flavors can provide comfort and relaxation, helping you ease into rest mode.

3. When You're Feeling Anxious: Find Your Grounding

Anxiety can make you feel scattered or overwhelmed, so finding grounding activities is essential to bring you back to the present moment. Here are some ways to calm your mind and center yourself.

The 5-4-3-2-1 Technique:
This grounding exercise helps you focus on the present. Look around and name five things you can see, four things you can touch, three things you can hear, two things you can smell, and one thing you can taste.

Hold an Object that Feels Comforting:
Sometimes, holding something familiar and comforting, like a soft blanket or a small keepsake, can help soothe anxiety. Focus on its texture, weight, and feel.

Try Gentle Yoga:
Simple yoga poses, such as child's pose, cat-cow, or forward fold, help release physical tension and quiet your mind. Take deep breaths and focus on each movement.

Write a List of Positive Affirmations:
Write down affirmations that make you feel safe, calm, and in control. You can even repeat them out loud if that feels right – it's a powerful way to shift anxious thoughts.

4. When You're Feeling Lonely: Connect and Nurture

Loneliness can be tough, but there are ways to bring connection and warmth into your day, even if you're by yourself. Here are some ideas to help you feel more connected and uplifted.

Call or Text a Friend or Family Member:
Reach out to someone you trust and let them know you're thinking of them. Sometimes, a quick chat or even a thoughtful text can make you feel less alone.

Write a Letter to Yourself:
Take some time to write a compassionate letter to yourself. Express understanding, encouragement, and remind yourself that it's okay to feel lonely sometimes.

Volunteer or Help Someone Out:
Helping others can create a sense of purpose and connection. Whether it's offering to run an errand for a neighbor or helping out at a local shelter, acts of kindness boost your mood.

Watch a Comforting Movie or Show:
Sometimes, watching a favorite movie or series feels like spending time with old friends. Choose something uplifting that brings a smile to your face.

5. When You're Feeling Bored: Spark Some Joy and Creativity

Boredom can lead to restlessness, but it's also an opportunity to try something new or revisit old hobbies. Here are some fun self-care ideas to beat boredom and spark a little joy.

Try a New Recipe:
Find a recipe you've been curious about and give it a try. Cooking can be a creative way to engage your senses and break up the routine.

Do a Creative Craft:
Try painting, drawing, or making a DIY project. Even if you're not an artist, letting yourself be creative without judgment can be very refreshing.

Learn a Few New Phrases in a Different Language:
Pick a language you like and learn a few common phrases. It's fun, stimulating, and may come in handy someday.

Dance Like No One's Watching:
Put on a favorite song and dance around your room. It's a fun, lighthearted way to boost your mood and shake off boredom.

6. When You're Feeling Unmotivated: Get Moving, Little by Little

When motivation is low, sometimes all it takes is a small action to get you moving. Here are some gentle self-care activities to boost your energy without pressure.

Break Tasks into Tiny Steps: If there's something you need to do but feel unmotivated, break it down into very small steps. Start with a single action – often, taking that first step can lead to more.

Take a Walk Outside:
A short walk in the fresh air can refresh your mind and give you a burst of energy. Look around, notice the sights and sounds, and let the movement invigorate you.

Clean One Small Space:
Pick a small area like your desk or a kitchen drawer and tidy it up. Decluttering a little space can give you a quick win and might even motivate you to keep going.

Listen to an Uplifting Podcast:
Find a podcast episode that interests or inspires you. Sometimes hearing new ideas and perspectives is just what you need to regain motivation.

7. When You're Feeling Inspired: Dive into Your Passions

When inspiration strikes, embrace it! This is a perfect time to nurture your creativity and passion. Here are ways to let your inspired self shine.

Start a Passion Project:
Whether it's writing, painting, or designing, use this inspired energy to start a new project. Let your imagination run wild without worrying about the end result.

Read a Book That Inspires You:
Find a book that aligns with your interests or goals, whether it's a memoir, a how-to guide, or even poetry. Let the words fuel your inspiration.

Make a Vision Board:
Collect images, quotes, and ideas that represent your dreams and goals. Arrange them on a poster or digital board for a visual reminder of what you're working towards.

Set Some New Goals:
With inspiration flowing, take a few minutes to set achievable goals. Break them down into steps, so you have a plan for making your inspiration last.

8. When You're Feeling Happy: Celebrate and Spread Joy

Happiness is meant to be celebrated! When you're in a good mood, take a moment to bask in it and spread that joy around. Here are some fun ways to celebrate your happy moments.

Make a "Happiness Playlist":
Compile a list of your favorite feel-good songs, so you can play them anytime you need a boost. Music can amplify your joy and make a good mood even better.

Share Your Happiness with Others:
Send a cheerful text, compliment someone, or just share a funny story. When you're happy, it's the perfect time to brighten someone else's day.

Take Photos or Write About It:
Document happy moments with photos or journal entries. Looking back on these later can bring joy, and it's a wonderful way to remember special times.

Do Something Fun, Just Because:
Treat yourself to something that makes you happy, whether it's a dessert, a favorite activity, or a little splurge. Celebrating joy is its own form of self-care.

Self-care is about honoring your needs, whatever they might be in the moment. By tuning into how you're feeling, you can choose activities that truly nourish you. Remember, self-care is personal, so feel free to mix and match these ideas and create a routine that fits your unique needs.

Chapter 9: The Power of Positive Habits

Creating positive habits can transform your daily life, making it easier to achieve your goals, feel more balanced, and build resilience. This chapter dives into the science of habits, offering practical ways to develop routines that support your well-being. Whether it's adding a small mindfulness practice, a gratitude ritual, or an energizing morning routine, here's how to make positive habits stick – and make them work for you.

1. Start Small:
Building Micro-Habits for Success

Big goals can feel overwhelming, but breaking them down into tiny, manageable habits makes them achievable and helps build momentum over time. Here's how to get started:

Identify Your End Goal: What is it that you ultimately want to achieve? Whether it's better physical health, less stress, or more organization, identify a clear goal to aim for.

Break It Down into Micro-Habits: Take your end goal and divide it into small, specific actions. For example, if you want to be more physically active, start with 5 minutes of movement each day rather than an hour-long workout.

Attach It to an Existing Habit: Pair your new habit with a routine you already have. For instance, do 5 minutes of stretching right after you brush your teeth in the morning. This pairing, known as habit stacking, makes new behaviors easier to remember.

Celebrate Small Wins: Acknowledge each small accomplishment. Whether it's keeping up with a daily task for a week or simply taking the first step, small celebrations help reinforce your new habit.

2. Morning Routines: Start the Day with Intention

A consistent morning routine can set a positive tone for the entire day, helping you feel organized, energized, and ready to face whatever comes your way. Here are some ideas for creating a routine that works for you:

Hydrate First Thing: Start with a glass of water to rehydrate your body after sleep. Adding a slice of lemon can add flavor and boost your morning hydration.

Practice Mindfulness or Gratitude: Take a few minutes to sit quietly, meditate, or write down three things you're grateful for. These practices can lift your mood and bring focus to the day.

Move Your Body: Gentle stretching, yoga, or even a short walk can wake up your body and improve circulation, helping you feel energized.

Plan Your Day: Write a short to-do list or review your schedule to prioritize important tasks. This helps to reduce stress by giving you a clear sense of purpose.

3. Evening Wind-Down:
Creating a Calming Night Routine

A good night's sleep starts long before you close your eyes. Building a calming night routine can help you wind down, release stress, and prepare your mind and body for rest.

Disconnect from Screens: Try to power down devices at least an hour before bed. The blue light from screens can interfere with your body's production of melatonin, making it harder to fall asleep.

Try Journaling or Reflection: Write about your day, list any worries, or reflect on positive moments. Journaling before bed can help you process thoughts and let go of any lingering stress.

Create a Soothing Environment: Dim the lights, play relaxing music, or light a candle to signal to your mind that it's time to wind down.

Practice Deep Breathing or Meditation: Spend a few minutes on deep breathing exercises or a short meditation to relax your body and clear your mind.

4. Building a Gratitude Practice

Regular gratitude practice is one of the most effective ways to boost happiness and resilience. Practicing gratitude helps shift focus away from stressors and reminds you of the positive aspects of life.

Start a Gratitude Journal:
Each day, write down three things you're grateful for. It could be something as simple as a good meal or a conversation that made you smile.

Express Gratitude to Others:
Make it a habit to thank people who impact your life. This could be in person, through a quick text, or even by writing a letter. Expressing gratitude strengthens connections and fosters positivity.

Do a Weekly Reflection:
At the end of each week, reflect on the highlights. Summing up your favorite moments, successes, or lessons helps reinforce gratitude and allows you to end the week on a positive note.

5. Physical Health Habits: Small Changes, Big Impact

Improving physical health doesn't require drastic measures – small changes can have a big impact over time. Here are some healthy habits that are easy to incorporate into your day:

Stay Hydrated Throughout the Day: Make hydration a priority. Keep a water bottle with you as a reminder, and try to drink a little water every hour.

Incorporate Movement into Your Routine: Even if you don't have time for a full workout, find ways to move more. Take the stairs, stretch every hour, or go for a quick walk during breaks.

Eat Mindfully: Eating slowly and savoring each bite can improve digestion and help you enjoy your meals more. Try not to multitask during meals – instead, focus on the flavors and textures of your food.

Prioritize Sleep: Good sleep is crucial for overall health. Aim for 7-8 hours of quality rest by keeping a consistent bedtime, limiting caffeine in the evening, and creating a relaxing pre-sleep routine.

6. Mental Health Habits: Nurturing a Healthy Mindset

Caring for your mental health is just as important as physical health. Here are some daily habits to keep your mind resilient, positive, and clear.

Practice Positive Self-Talk: Pay attention to your inner dialogue. When you catch yourself in negative self-talk, try to reframe it with kinder words. For example, replace "I'm so bad at this" with "I'm still learning, and that's okay."

Limit News and Social Media: Staying informed is important, but overexposure to news and social media can increase stress. Set boundaries around screen time, and be mindful of how it affects your mood.

Make Time for Hobbies: Engaging in activities you enjoy boosts mood and reduces stress. Whether it's painting, reading, gardening, or cooking, spending time on hobbies nurtures your creativity and well-being.

Check In with Yourself: Take a few moments each day to assess your emotions and energy levels. Self-reflection can help you better understand your needs and make adjustments as needed.

7. Cultivating Mindfulness and Presence

Mindfulness is the practice of being fully present in the moment. It helps reduce stress, increase awareness, and deepen your connection to yourself and others. Here's how to incorporate mindfulness into your daily life:

Set Aside 5 Minutes for Meditation:
Even a few minutes of meditation each day can improve focus and reduce stress. Sit quietly, focus on your breath, and gently return your focus if your mind starts to wander.

Engage Fully in Routine Activities:
Bring mindfulness to everyday activities like washing dishes or brushing your teeth. Pay attention to the sensations, sounds, and smells. This practice can transform mundane moments into peaceful, grounding experiences.

Take Mindful Breaks:
Throughout the day, take a few moments to close your eyes, breathe deeply, and just be. Mindful breaks can reset your energy and keep you feeling balanced.

8. The Power of Saying "No" and Setting Boundaries

Setting healthy boundaries is key to protecting your time and energy. Learning to say "no" can be challenging, but it's essential for maintaining balance and avoiding burnout.

Identify Your Priorities:

Knowing your values and priorities makes it easier to say "no" when something doesn't align with them. Reflect on what truly matters to you and use this as a guide.

Practice Saying "No" Respectfully:

Saying "no" doesn't have to be uncomfortable. Try phrases like "I appreciate the offer, but I won't be able to" or "Thanks for thinking of me, but I need some time for myself."

Limit Your Commitments: Resist the urge to overcommit. Start by setting boundaries with smaller tasks or social invitations, and gradually work toward bigger ones.

Honor Your Boundaries: Once you set a boundary, stick to it. Remind yourself that respecting your limits is a form of self-care and ultimately benefits your well-being.

9. The Habit of Self-Compassion

Being kind to yourself, especially during challenging times, is a powerful habit. Self-compassion means treating yourself with the same kindness you'd offer to a friend, fostering resilience and emotional well-being.

Speak Kindly to Yourself: Practice talking to yourself with gentle, supportive words. When you're hard on yourself, imagine what you'd say to a friend in the same situation and apply that kindness to yourself.

Accept Mistakes as Part of Growth: Mistakes are a natural part of life and learning. Instead of criticizing yourself, view them as opportunities for growth and self-discovery.

Give Yourself Permission to Rest: Self-compassion includes recognizing when you need rest and giving yourself permission to take a break. Remember that rest is productive and necessary.

Practice Forgiving Yourself: Holding onto regret can be heavy. Remind yourself that it's okay to let go and that forgiving yourself allows you to move forward.

Chapter 10: Holiday Word Search – Find the Festive Words

Holiday word searches are a classic activity to enjoy the season's magic. In this chapter, you'll find Word Search sheets packed with holiday-themed words.

How to Play Holiday Word Search

Find the Words: Search for each word listed next to the puzzle grid. Words can be hidden horizontally, vertically, diagonally, or even backward within the grid.

Circle or Highlight: Once you find a word, circle or highlight it directly on the Word Search sheet to keep track.

Cross Off the List: After circling a word, cross it off the list so you know which words are left to find.

Optional Challenge: Try timing yourself to see how quickly you can complete each puzzle or compete with friends and family to add a little friendly holiday competition.

Each Word Search sheet offers a cozy, mindful activity that's perfect for a holiday break. These puzzles are fun for all ages and a great way to enjoy holiday-inspired words, perfect for relaxing with a warm drink.

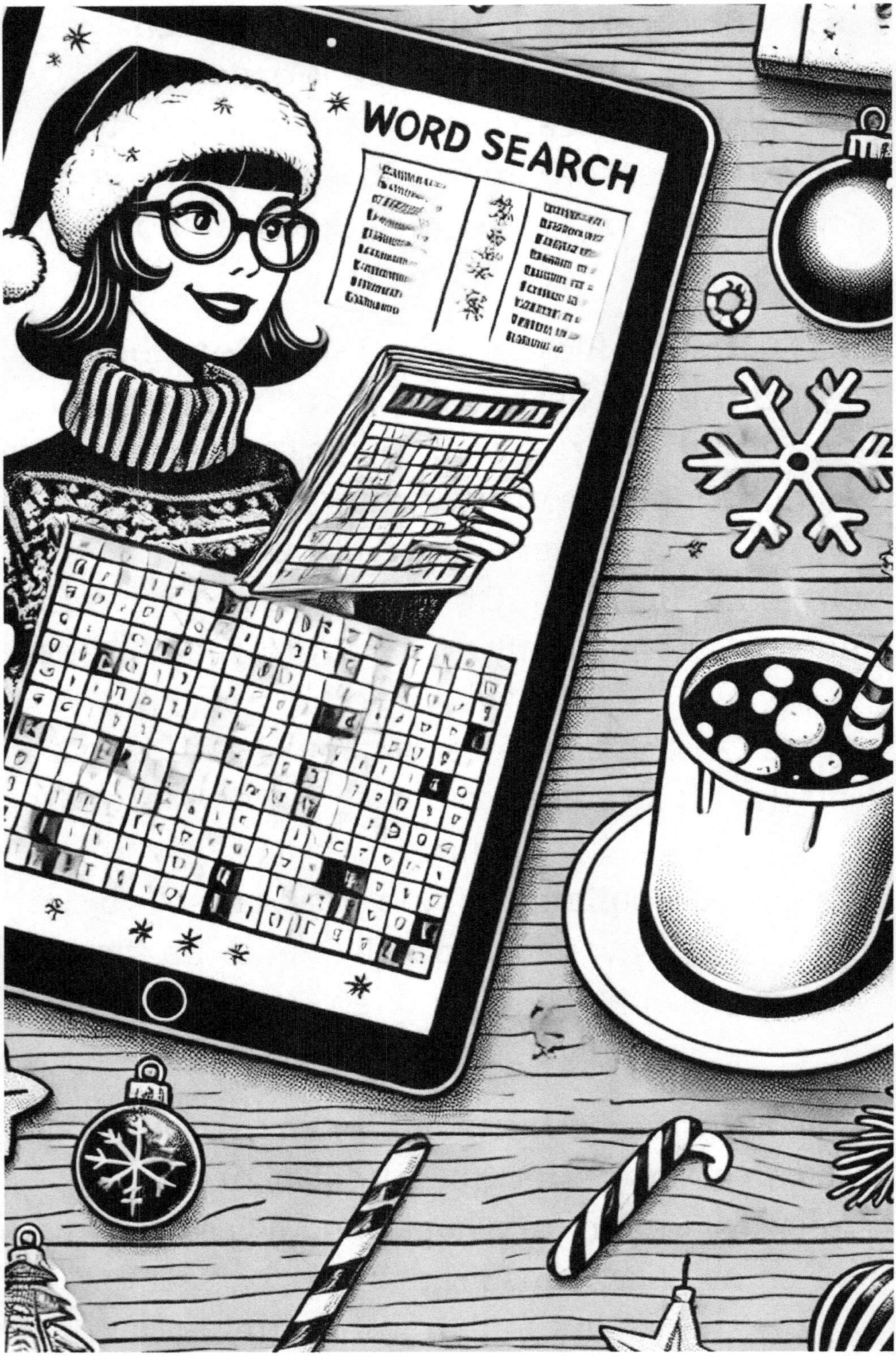
WORD SEARCH

Christmas Kitchen

```
N U M U F F I N S F I I
I I L N C M T S E F L O
E I C A F O U O L T E L
I O N T R I L G U G C A
T E A P O T G G N E T A
N K C I I N S C T N F A
E O P N R L S O I N K N
T N U T M E G N I K A B
T O M P I T L T G I I A
A O G K E C M F N I I I
L R O C E O T O I E P G
N O O L I C N U C R N A
C I L T P O N I I O T T
E C I N N A M O N I C E
G N I T S A O R C C A M
I I N T T G I T T T P O
```

Words List

Cookies	Cinnamon	Nutmeg
Baking	Trifle	Roasting
Icing	Muffins	Pie
Cocoa	Teapot	Latte

2 Winter Wonderland Woman

```
T S L O T L G C O H L S
I K C T L K S R A C T C
C A C S C R T L I P L A
P R Y G N A S S T E F N
T N Z E S O N O O I N L
E O O A N A W D L R O U
N I C E E I F F L S F F
S E L T T S O O A E Z I
N R N T T E R R I L S R
O S D O I I K T E N L E
E T O H M E P N N E A P
S R E P P I L S A G I L
G N I D A E R N P L L A
K T L Z G P P U O S B C
T T O N I A H T L A A E
S O A G N I T T I N K W
```

Words List

Snowfall	Frost	Mittens
Fireplace	Blanket	Slippers
Candles	Knitting	Reading
Cozy	Soup	Hot Tea

Winter Beauty Routine

H C O N D I T I O N I S
I A I L M T I L I I E Z
F S N M O B N L T T T K
O E N O I T L I K I A S
E S R L S T I U S E I A
L N P L T E T O S R L M
I R N A U A F E N H O R
P C E O R T L L N M F E
B L E R I K P N Z S X Z
A E R A Z N L B T B E N
L A C O E E R E I I T O
M N S O Z H O I N R M R
U S N O B E O S S H S B
A E U L T M K I O B T U
A R S A C L O E E T N S
S O S L E O E L N S R O

Words List

Moisturize	Lip Balm	Sparkle
Blush	Mittens	Exfoliate
Mask	Condition	Cleanser
Lotion	Sunscreen	Bronzer

4   Christmas Day Spa

```
E Y B S E N O T S T O H
E R M O C R B P I C G M
R U E O R I U S C R U B
A U S D E S B C B S U T
M E E B B B B D I H B C
A U M B M T L R T D U R
S X C P U E E E T B E E
S M A S C L B K A L R P
A A M L U R A U A M K S
G E U M C F T X A A A S
E T D B G B H E T L B T
E S M A F A C I A L A M
Y P A R E H T A M O R A
C S S R A O E B S T G E
E L K B R B O I L S A R
R S D N M D N S T L U U
```

Words List

Bubble Bath	Pedicure	Facial
Relax	Aromatherapy	Mud Mask
Massage	Scrub	Oils
Steam	Hot Stones	Cucumber

Jewelry Box Joys

```
R S R S R B A E N N G E
E E D E C H C A A A A R
K C L A N E L M G N I R
O B C R O U E S E S U L
H T M R A H C O C E L T
C K R I G T E U N O O N
A C D N T S T S E R N A
L K K G L G D D C H P D
K O O S N G S K K R N N
D H C O O R B S L K R E
O R L K A A K K A A D P
B R A C E L E T C N C K
R N P O A T S R E K C A
K A P K E H G N E L R B
E R O S T U D S C E E R
E L G N A B O U E T N N
```

Words List

Locket	Bracelet	Earrings
Ring	Brooch	Necklace
Anklet	Pendant	Bangle
Studs	Choker	Charm

Holiday Self-Care

```
P A A D H M A N D E X A
E S A E R M A S S A G E
N D D K G M T E T S S H
T R S X M H E X R E T E
H Y D R A T E E A D R E
S M G T D O R T T E E K
C A D A N C E T T E T I
G N S E H I E I I E C H
I I H A G R A D E D H A
R C E N U H E E D E I E
D U X P A I N T E N T A
T R T T L T N O P S O D
P E T S I U U X U E A U
S D A U A I P R A N T D
P E D I C U R E E T R E
A H U G C D N E T E T C
```

Words List

Massage	Nature	Laugh
Dance	Stretch	Paint
Hydrate	Detox	Manicure
Pedicure	Hike	Dream

1 Solution

```
N U M U F F I N S F I I
I I L N C M T S E F L O
E I C A F O U O L T E L
I O N T R I L G U G C A
T E A P O T G G N E T A
N K C I I N S C T N F A
E O P N R L S O I N K N
T N U T M E G N I K A B
T O M P I T L T G I I A
A O G K E C M F N I I I
L R O C E O T O I E P G
N O O L I C N U C R N A
C I L T P O N I I O T T
E C I N N A M O N I C E
G N I T S A O R C C A M
I I N T T G I T T T P O
```

2 Solution

```
T S L O T L G C O H L S
I K C T L K S R A C T C
C A C S C R T L I P L A
P R Y G N A S T E F N
T N Z E S O N O O I N L
E O O A N A W D L R O U
N I C E E I F F L S F F
S E L T T S O O A E Z I
N R N T T E R R I L S R
O S D O I I K T E N L E
E T O H M E P N N E A P
S R E P P I L S A G I L
G N I D A E R N P L L A
K T L Z G P P U O S B C
T T O N I A H T L A A E
S O A G N I T T I N K W
```

3 Solution

```
H C O N D I T I O N I S
I A I L M T I L I I E Z
F S N M O B N L T T T K
O E N O I T L I K I A S
E S R L S T I U S E I A
L N P L T E T O S R L M
I R N A U A F E N H O R
P C E O R T L L N M F E
B L E R I K P N Z S X Z
A E R A Z N L B T B E N
L A C O E E R E I I T O
M N S O Z H O I N R M R
U S N O B E O S S H S B
A E U L T M K I O B T U
A R S A C L O E E T N S
S O S L E O E L N S R O
```

4 Solution

```
E Y B S E N O T S T O H
E R M O C R B P I C G M
R U E O R I U S C R U B
A U S D E S B C B S U T
M E E B B B B D I H B C
A U M B M T L R T D U R
S X C P U E E E T B E E
S M A S C L B K A L R P
A A M L U R A U A M K S
G E U M C F T X A A A S
E T D B G B H E T L B T
E S M A F A C I A L A M
Y P A R E H T A M O R A
C S S R A O E B S T G E
E L K B R B O I L S A R
R S D N M D N S T L U U
```

5 Solution

R	S	R	S	R	B	A	E	N	N	G	E
E	E	D	E	C	H	C	A	A	A	A	R
K	C	L	A	N	E	L	M	G	N	I	R
O	B	C	R	O	U	E	S	E	S	U	L
H	T	M	R	A	H	C	O	C	E	L	T
C	K	R	I	G	T	E	U	N	O	O	N
A	C	D	N	T	S	T	S	E	R	N	A
L	K	K	G	L	G	D	D	C	H	P	D
K	O	O	S	N	G	S	K	K	R	N	N
D	H	C	O	O	R	B	S	L	K	R	E
O	R	L	K	A	A	K	K	A	A	D	P
B	R	A	C	E	L	E	T	C	N	C	K
R	N	P	O	A	T	S	R	E	K	C	A
K	A	P	K	E	H	G	N	E	L	R	B
E	R	O	S	T	U	D	S	C	E	E	R
E	L	G	N	A	B	O	U	E	T	N	N

6 Solution

P	A	A	D	H	M	A	N	D	E	X	A
E	S	A	E	R	M	A	S	S	A	G	E
N	D	D	K	G	M	T	E	T	S	S	H
T	R	S	X	M	H	E	X	R	E	T	E
H	Y	D	R	A	T	E	E	A	D	R	E
S	M	G	T	D	O	R	T	T	E	E	K
C	A	D	A	N	C	E	T	T	E	T	I
G	N	S	E	H	I	E	I	I	E	C	H
I	I	H	A	G	R	A	D	E	D	H	A
R	C	E	N	U	H	E	E	D	E	I	E
D	U	X	P	A	I	N	T	E	N	T	A
T	R	T	T	L	T	N	O	P	S	O	D
P	E	T	S	I	U	U	X	U	E	A	U
S	D	A	U	A	I	P	R	A	N	T	D
P	E	D	I	C	U	R	E	E	T	R	E
A	H	U	G	C	D	N	E	T	E	T	C

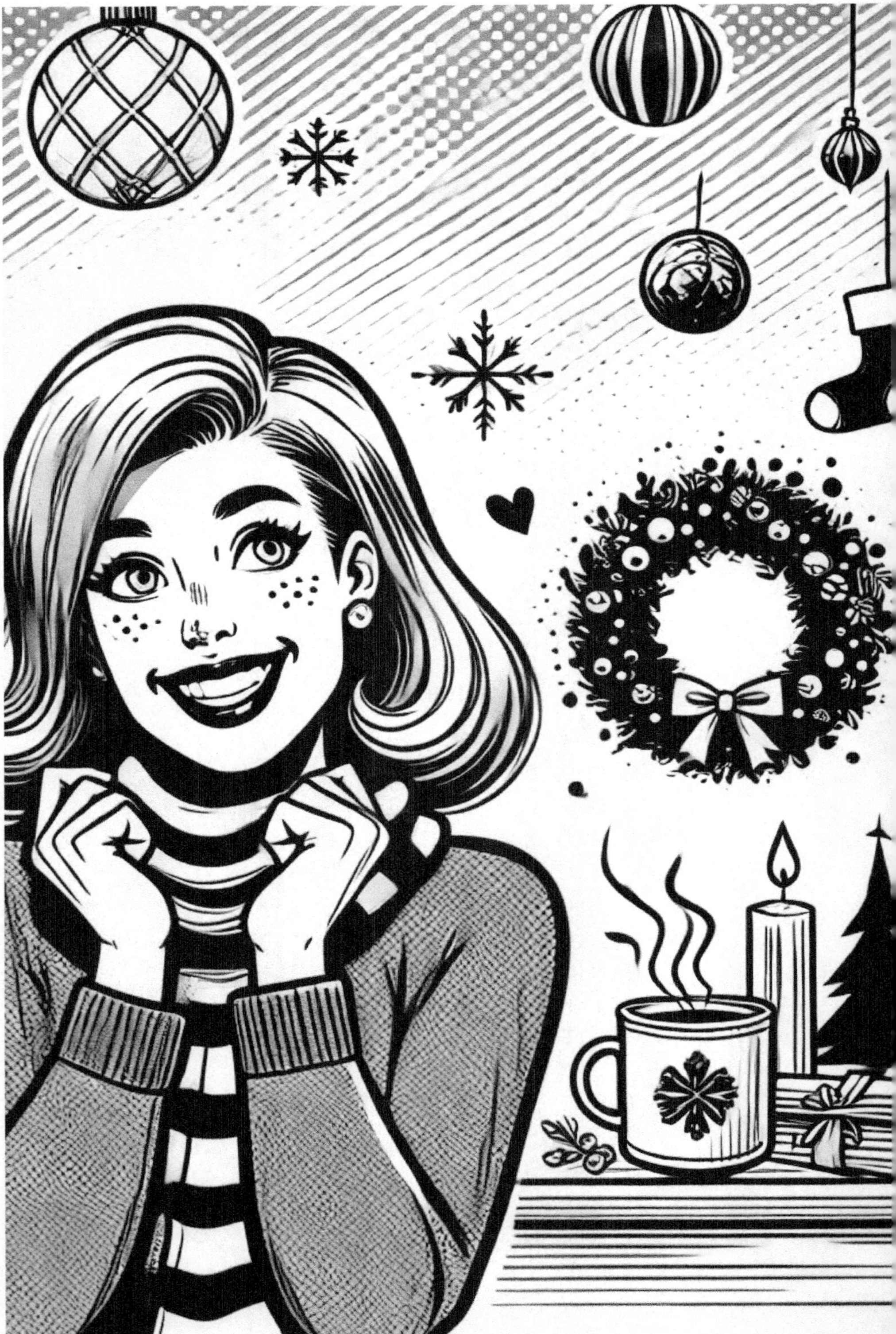

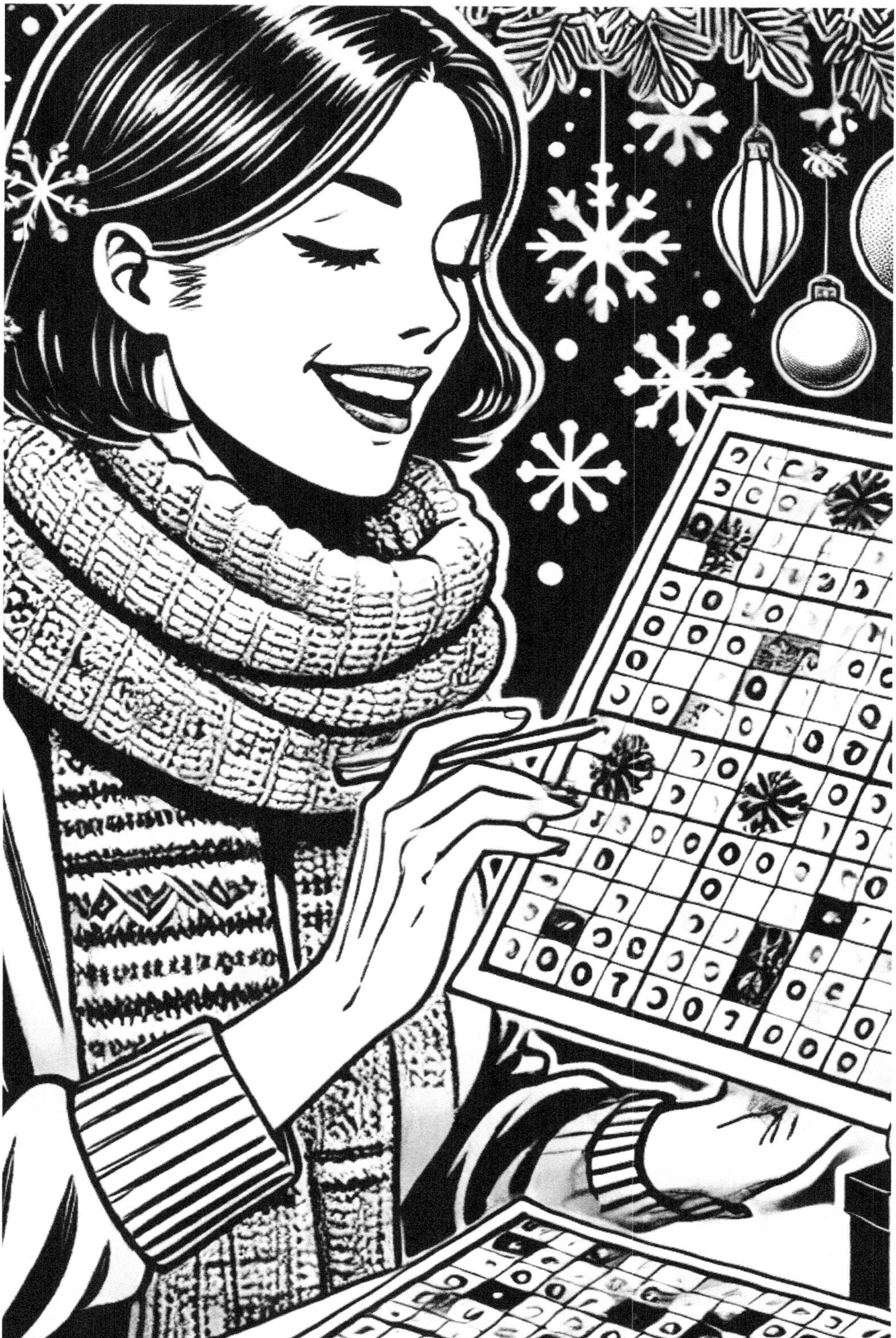

Chapter 11: Christmas Sudoku – A Seasonal Challenge

Christmas-themed Sudoku is a festive way to relax and stay sharp. This chapter offers puzzles from easy to advanced, so all skill levels can enjoy.

How to Play Christmas Sudoku

Objective: Fill each 9x9 grid with numbers 1 to 9. Ensure each row, column, and 3x3 box has no repeats.

Use Clues: Each puzzle has some numbers pre-filled to help you start.

Apply Logic: Use logic to place numbers. Check each row, column, and box to narrow down options.

Take Your Time: Sudoku requires patience. If stuck, take a break and return refreshed.

Challenge Levels: Start with easy puzzles, then move to harder ones as you gain confidence.

These Christmas Sudoku sheets are perfect for a cozy holiday break, combining relaxation with a touch of mental challenge!

EASY 01

1	7			3		6	5	2
5		3	1	2	6			7
6	2		5	4	7	1	9	3
		6	7	9			1	5
	3	1	6	5		8	4	9
4	5	9		8	1	7	2	6
9	6	7	2		8	5	3	4
8	4		9			2	7	
3	1	2	4	7	5	9	6	8

EASY 02

	2	6	5	4	9	1	8	7
	1	8	2	6	3		9	4
	5	4				3		6
5	3	1		8	6	2	7	9
4	7	9		5			1	
6	8		9		7	4	5	3
2	4	3	8	9		7	6	5
	6	5	7		4		3	1
1	9	7		3	5	8	4	

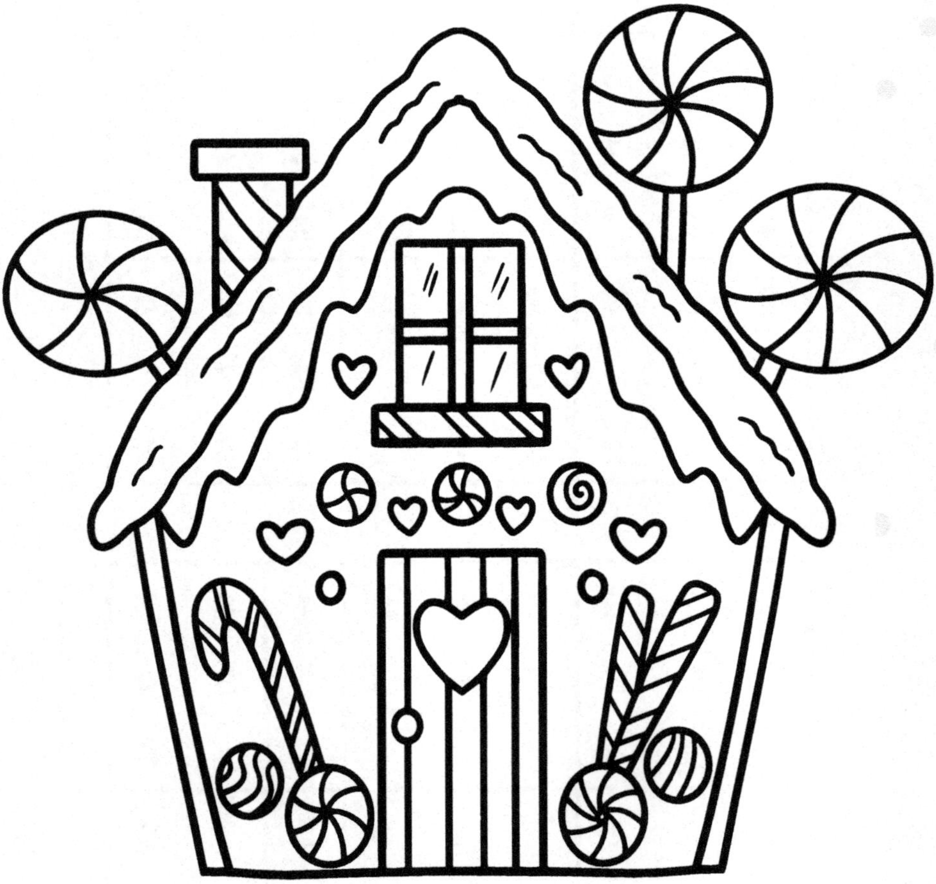

EASY 03

3	4	1	7			6	8	9
7	5		6	9	3		4	2
6	9	2	1	8	4	3		5
1		9	8	7	6	2		4
2	8	7						6
4	6	5	2			7	1	
9	7	3	5	2	8			1
	1			6	7		2	3
8	2	6			1	5	9	

EASY 04

	3		1	5	9			
		9		6	4	3	1	
1	4	6	3		7	9	2	
8	7	4	6	2	3	1	5	
6	2	5		9	1	7	3	
		1	8	7	5		6	4
3	5	1	9	4			7	2
4	6	2		3	8	5	9	1
7		8	5	1	2		4	3

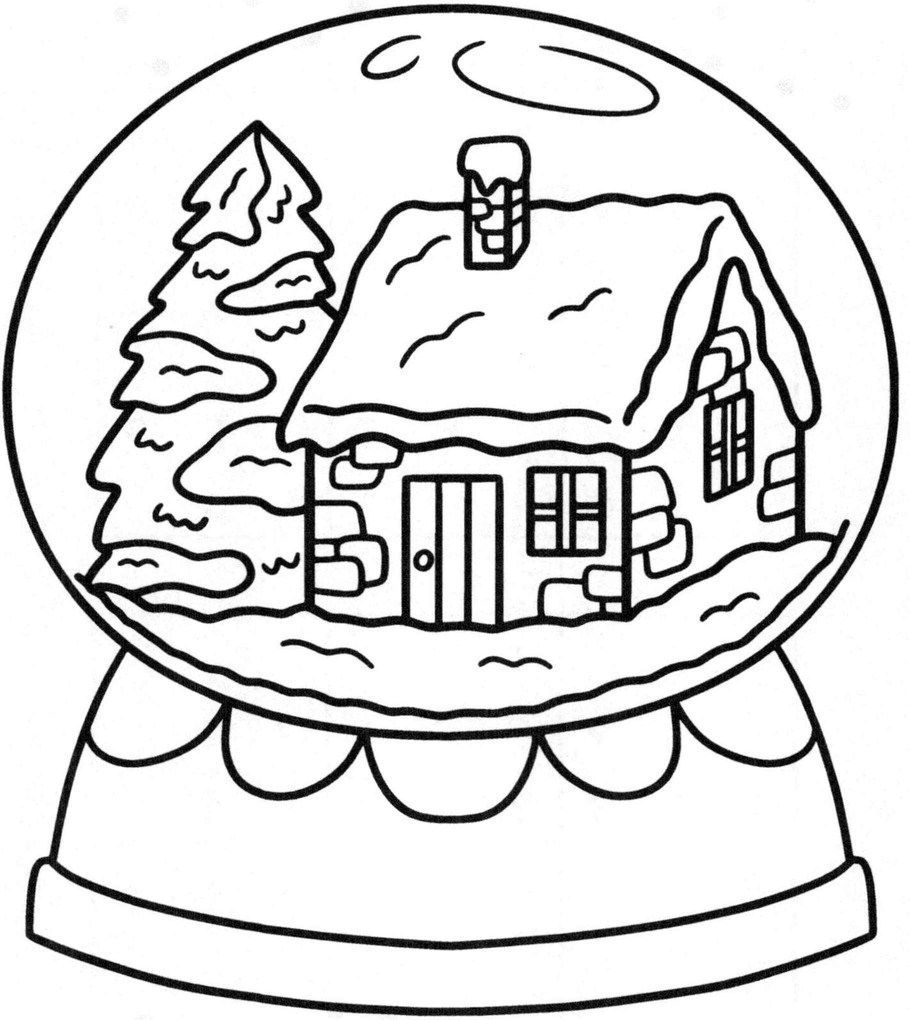

MEDIUM 01

7	4		9			5	3	6
3		6			4		7	8
	9	5	3		6			
			4		5	2	6	
4	6	7	8	2	9	3	5	
	5				7	8		
		9	5				4	
	7	4	2	9		1		5
5	1	3	7	4	8	6	2	9

MEDIUM 02

			2	1	5	8		3
			4	9	6		5	7
	2		8	7				
9	5	7	3		2	1		8
	3	4			1		7	
1	8	2	7		9	6	3	
	4	1			7	3		6
			6	3	4		8	1
	6			2		5	9	4

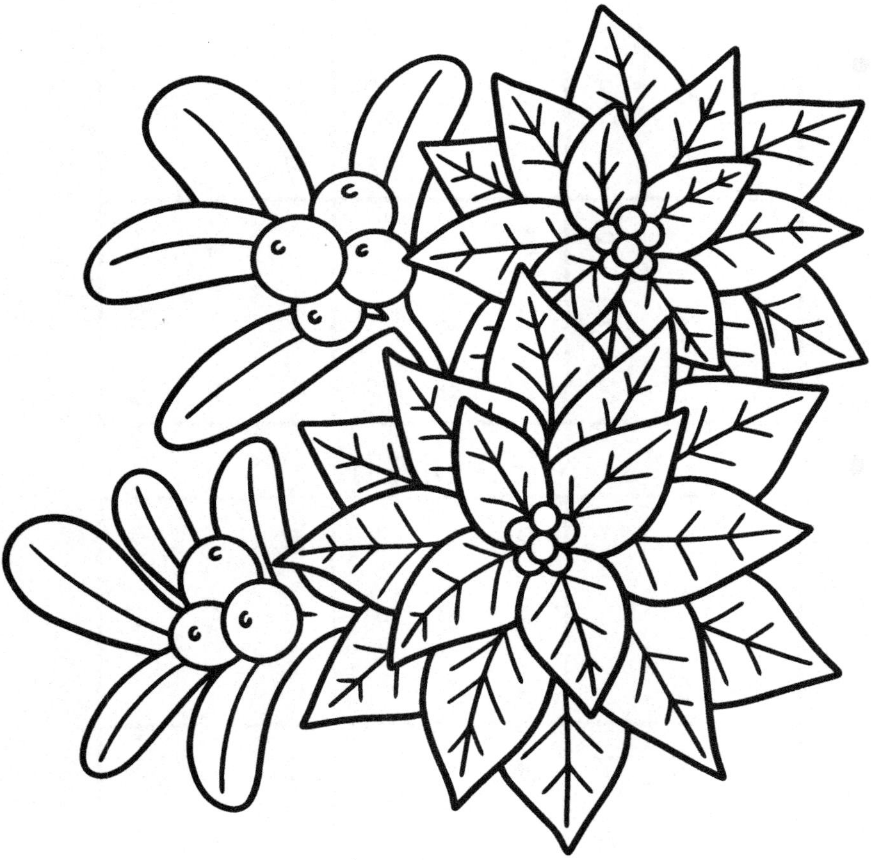

MEDIUM 03

6		5			8			9
9	2	3				8	6	7
8		4	3	6			5	1
1		6	9		4			2
4			2	5	7	6		8
7	5	2	8	1	6	9	3	4
2	4			8	3		9	5
	9	8			5	4	2	
			4	9	2	7		3

MEDIUM 04

	6	9		8		7	4	
	1	8	2	7	4		9	3
4	3	7		6	9	8	2	1
	5		9	2	8	1	7	
7	8						3	
1		2		4	7	5	6	8
8	4	6		9	1			
							1	
	2	1		5	6	9		

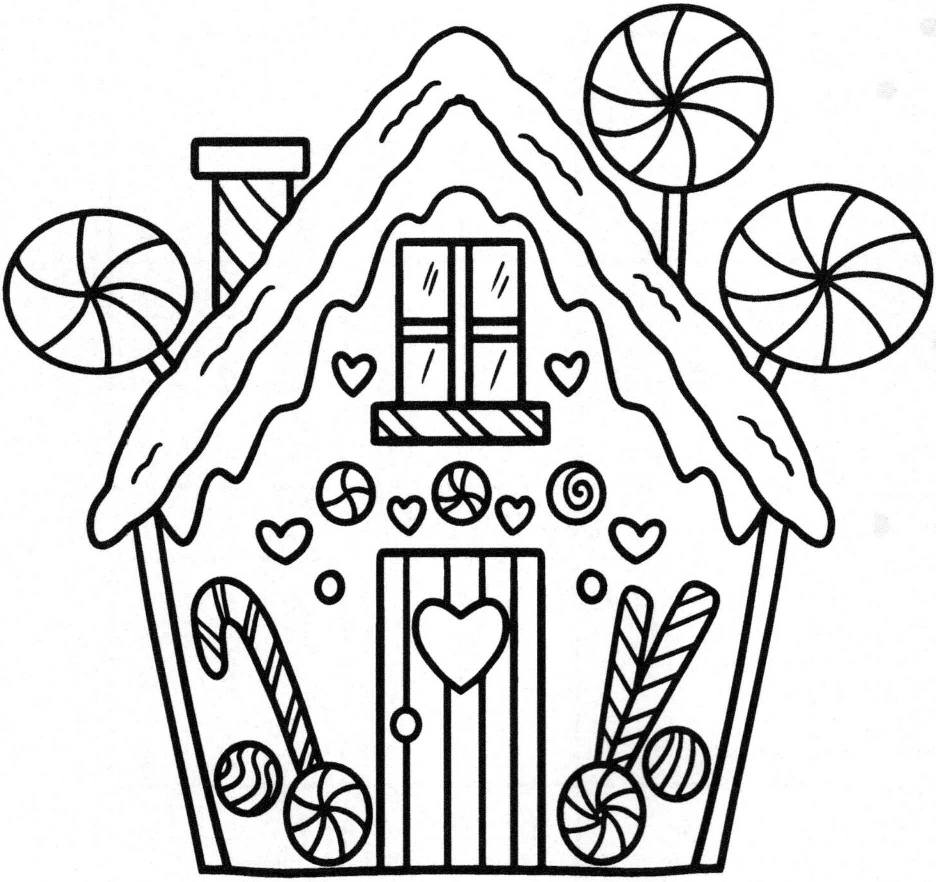

HARD 01

8		9				7	1	4
1			3	9			5	2
5			1	4	7	8	9	
					3	4		9
7					9		2	1
9		2		1				
	9		8			2		7
2			9	3		1	6	
		6	8	2		1	4	

HARD 02

7			4			6	1	
9	4			1	6	2	8	5
1		6				9		
4	6	1		8				9
2	9			3			6	8
	3	8		2			4	
6	5	9	2		1			7
8		4			5			
3				7				6

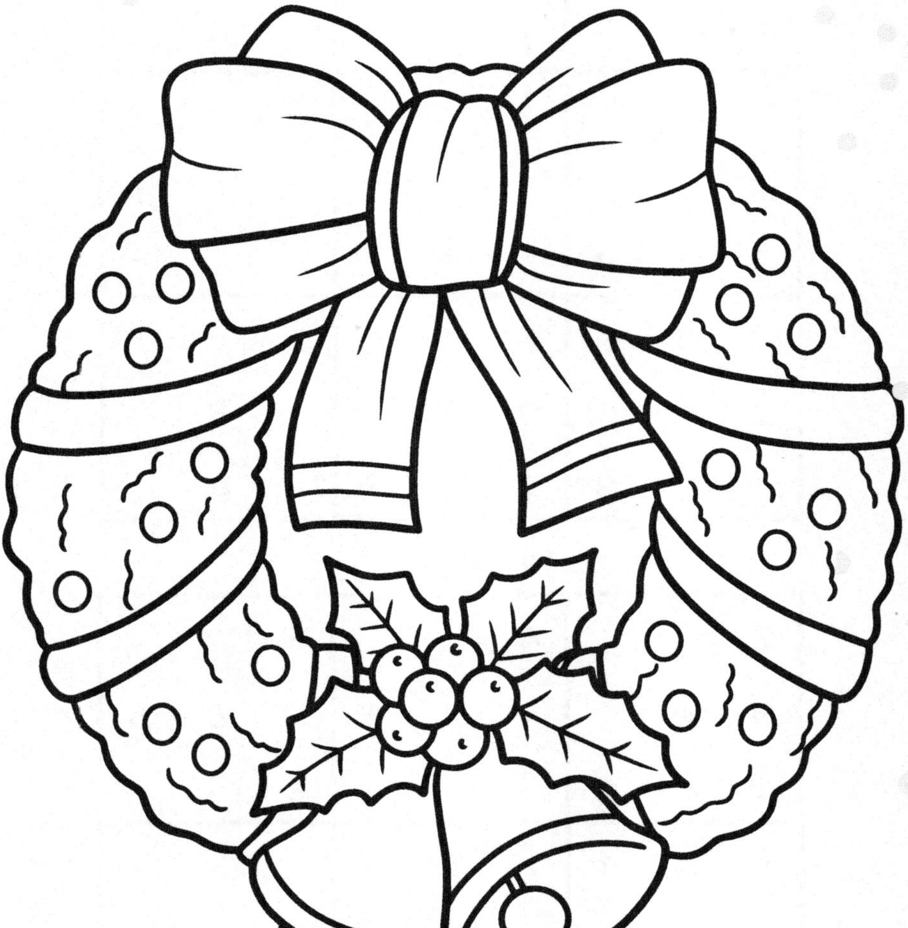

HARD 03

4	2	6	9			5		
	8				2			
				8		5	7		4
3	5		2	8		1	6	
6	1	9	3	5				
8	7	2	6				3	5
	4		7			9		
		5	1					2
2	9	3	5		8	6	1	

HARD 04

3	5	9	2	4	6	7		
		1	9	3				6
		7			8			2
2	8		4	5	1			
	1		3	8	9	5	2	4
9	4		6	7			1	3
5								
	3	8	7	2		1		
		2	8					7

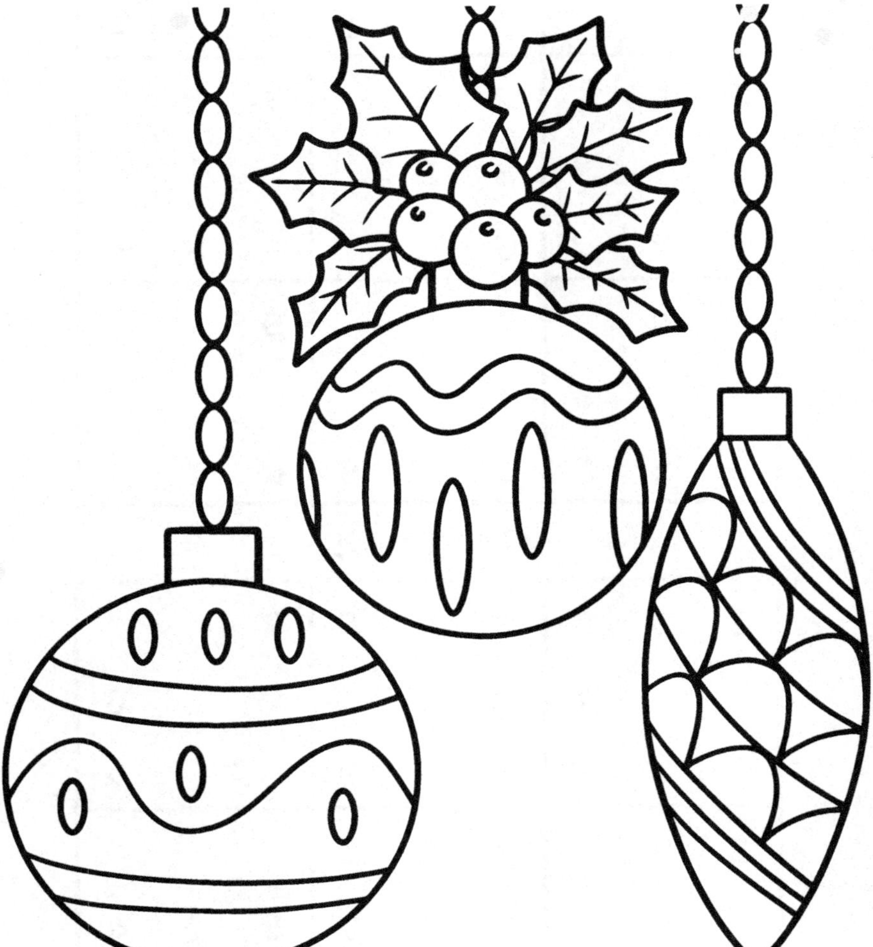

DIFFICULT 01

2					1	9		3
4		7					1	5
	9			4			7	
			7	8	5		9	1
		1						
	7		1	9	3		6	
	4					7	2	
	1		9				5	
	8		2	5		1		9

DIFFICULT 02

	9		3		5	2		
		5			1	3	9	
3	8	6		9	2		1	7
1		4	8	5		9		
				2		9		4	
	5						7	
	1		9	2			8	6
			5	3		1		9
						4	5	

DIFFICULT 03

	4				6		8	
7	3		1					
		8	5	7		1	3	4
		5	6	2			1	8
				4	1		2	9
	7				8	3		
	5		8	9	1	2	7	
			3		4			
3				6				5

DIFFICULT 04

9	3						5	8
5	1		3	2				9
	4							
7			9	1	2		8	4
				5			9	2
3		9	6					7
2			4	3		6		
	5		8	9		2		
					5	8		1

Easy

Puzzle 01

1	7	4	8	3	9	6	5	2
5	9	3	1	2	6	4	8	7
6	2	8	5	4	7	1	9	3
2	8	6	7	9	4	3	1	5
7	3	1	6	5	2	8	4	9
4	5	9	3	8	1	7	2	6
9	6	7	2	1	8	5	3	4
8	4	5	9	6	3	2	7	1
3	1	2	4	7	5	9	6	8

Puzzle 02

3	2	6	5	4	9	1	8	7
7	1	8	2	6	3	5	9	4
9	5	4	1	7	8	3	2	6
5	3	1	4	8	6	2	7	9
4	7	9	3	5	2	6	1	8
6	8	2	9	1	7	4	5	3
2	4	3	8	9	1	7	6	5
8	6	5	7	2	4	9	3	1
1	9	7	6	3	5	8	4	2

Puzzle 03

3	4	1	7	5	2	6	8	9
7	5	8	6	9	3	1	4	2
6	9	2	1	8	4	3	7	5
1	3	9	8	7	6	2	5	4
2	8	7	4	1	5	9	3	6
4	6	5	2	3	9	7	1	8
9	7	3	5	2	8	4	6	1
5	1	4	9	6	7	8	2	3
8	2	6	3	4	1	5	9	7

Puzzle 04

2	3	7	1	5	9	4	8	6
5	8	9	2	6	4	3	1	7
1	4	6	3	8	7	9	2	5
8	7	4	6	2	3	1	5	9
6	2	5	4	9	1	7	3	8
9	1	3	8	7	5	2	6	4
3	5	1	9	4	6	8	7	2
4	6	2	7	3	8	5	9	1
7	9	8	5	1	2	6	4	3

Medium

Puzzle 01

7	4	1	9	8	2	5	3	6
3	2	6	1	5	4	9	7	8
8	9	5	3	7	6	4	1	2
9	3	8	4	1	5	2	6	7
4	6	7	8	2	9	3	5	1
1	5	2	6	3	7	8	9	4
2	8	9	5	6	1	7	4	3
6	7	4	2	9	3	1	8	5
5	1	3	7	4	8	6	2	9

Puzzle 02

4	7	9	2	1	5	8	6	3
3	1	8	4	9	6	2	5	7
5	2	6	8	7	3	4	1	9
9	5	7	3	6	2	1	4	8
6	3	4	5	8	1	9	7	2
1	8	2	7	4	9	6	3	5
8	4	1	9	5	7	3	2	6
2	9	5	6	3	4	7	8	1
7	6	3	1	2	8	5	9	4

Puzzle 03

6	1	5	7	2	8	3	4	9
9	2	3	5	4	1	8	6	7
8	7	4	3	6	9	2	5	1
1	8	6	9	3	4	5	7	2
4	3	9	2	5	7	6	1	8
7	5	2	8	1	6	9	3	4
2	4	7	6	8	3	1	9	5
3	9	8	1	7	5	4	2	6
5	6	1	4	9	2	7	8	3

Puzzle 04

2	6	9	1	8	3	7	4	5
5	1	8	2	7	4	6	9	3
4	3	7	5	6	9	8	2	1
6	5	3	9	2	8	1	7	4
7	8	4	6	1	5	2	3	9
1	9	2	3	4	7	5	6	8
8	4	6	7	9	1	3	5	2
9	7	5	8	3	2	4	1	6
3	2	1	4	5	6	9	8	7

Hard

Puzzle 01

8	3	9	5	6	2	7	1	4
1	7	4	3	9	8	6	5	2
5	2	6	1	4	7	8	9	3
6	1	5	7	2	3	4	8	9
7	4	3	6	8	9	5	2	1
9	8	2	4	1	5	3	7	6
4	9	1	8	5	6	2	3	7
2	5	7	9	3	4	1	6	8
3	6	8	2	7	1	9	4	5

Puzzle 02

7	8	5	4	9	2	6	1	3
9	4	3	7	1	6	2	8	5
1	2	6	8	5	3	9	7	4
4	6	1	5	8	7	3	2	9
2	9	7	1	3	4	5	6	8
5	3	8	6	2	9	7	4	1
6	5	9	2	4	1	8	3	7
8	7	4	3	6	5	1	9	2
3	1	2	9	7	8	4	5	6

Puzzle 03

4	2	6	9	7	3	5	8	1
5	8	7	4	1	2	3	9	6
9	3	1	8	6	5	7	2	4
3	5	4	2	8	7	1	6	9
6	1	9	3	5	4	2	7	8
8	7	2	6	9	1	4	3	5
1	4	8	7	2	6	9	5	3
7	6	5	1	3	9	8	4	2
2	9	3	5	4	8	6	1	7

Puzzle 04

3	5	9	2	4	6	7	8	1
8	2	1	9	3	7	4	5	6
4	6	7	5	1	8	9	3	2
2	8	3	4	5	1	6	7	9
7	1	6	3	8	9	5	2	4
9	4	5	6	7	2	8	1	3
5	7	4	1	9	3	2	6	8
6	3	8	7	2	4	1	9	5
1	9	2	8	6	5	3	4	7

Difficult

Puzzle 01

2	5	8	6	7	1	9	4	3
4	6	7	8	3	9	2	1	5
1	9	3	5	4	2	6	7	8
6	2	4	7	8	5	3	9	1
9	3	1	4	2	6	5	8	7
8	7	5	1	9	3	4	6	2
5	4	9	3	1	8	7	2	6
3	1	2	9	6	7	8	5	4
7	8	6	2	5	4	1	3	9

Puzzle 02

7	9	1	3	8	5	2	6	4
2	4	5	7	6	1	3	9	8
3	8	6	4	9	2	5	1	7
1	6	4	8	5	7	9	3	2
8	3	7	2	1	9	6	4	5
9	5	2	6	4	3	8	7	1
5	1	3	9	2	4	7	8	6
4	7	8	5	3	6	1	2	9
6	2	9	1	7	8	4	5	3

Puzzle 03

5	4	1	2	3	6	9	8	7
7	3	9	1	4	8	6	5	2
2	8	6	5	7	9	1	3	4
4	9	5	6	2	7	3	1	8
8	6	3	4	1	5	7	2	9
1	7	2	9	8	3	5	4	6
6	5	4	8	9	1	2	7	3
9	2	7	3	5	4	8	6	1
3	1	8	7	6	2	4	9	5

Puzzle 04

9	3	7	1	4	6	2	5	8
5	1	6	3	2	8	7	4	9
8	4	2	5	7	9	1	3	6
7	6	5	9	1	2	3	8	4
1	8	4	7	5	3	6	9	2
3	2	9	6	8	4	5	1	7
2	7	8	4	3	1	9	6	5
6	5	1	8	9	7	4	2	3
4	9	3	2	6	5	8	7	1

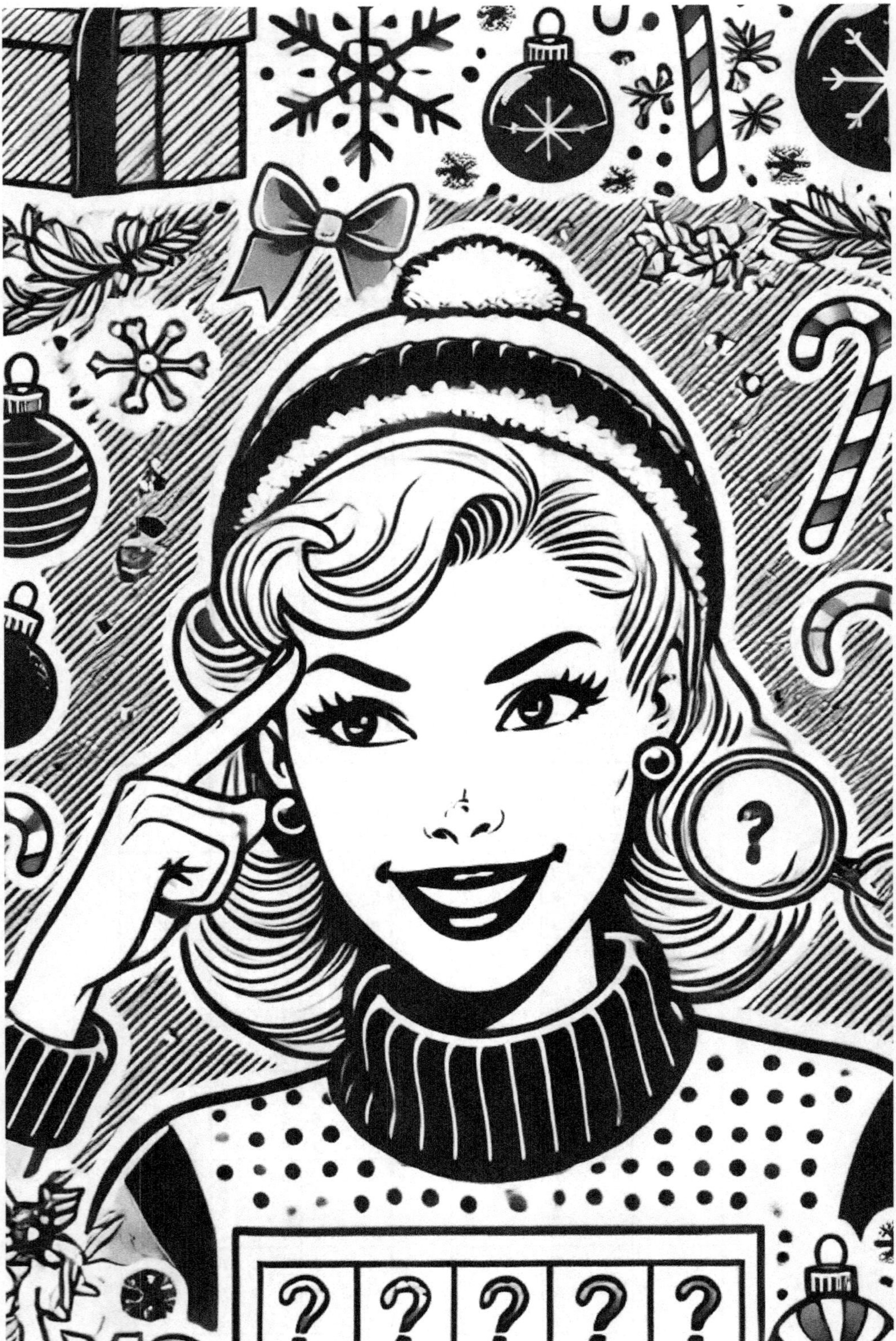

Chapter 12: Holiday Seek & Find – Discover the Hidden Treasures

Explore beautifully illustrated holiday scenes packed with hidden treasures to uncover. Each Seek & Find sheet features intricate holiday-themed artwork, with lists of specific items to locate, like candy canes, ornaments, or snowflakes.

Use these pages to test your observation skills while enjoying the charming holiday details. Take your time as you circle each hidden object, and enjoy a festive adventure on every page!

Search and Find

Search and Find

Search and Find

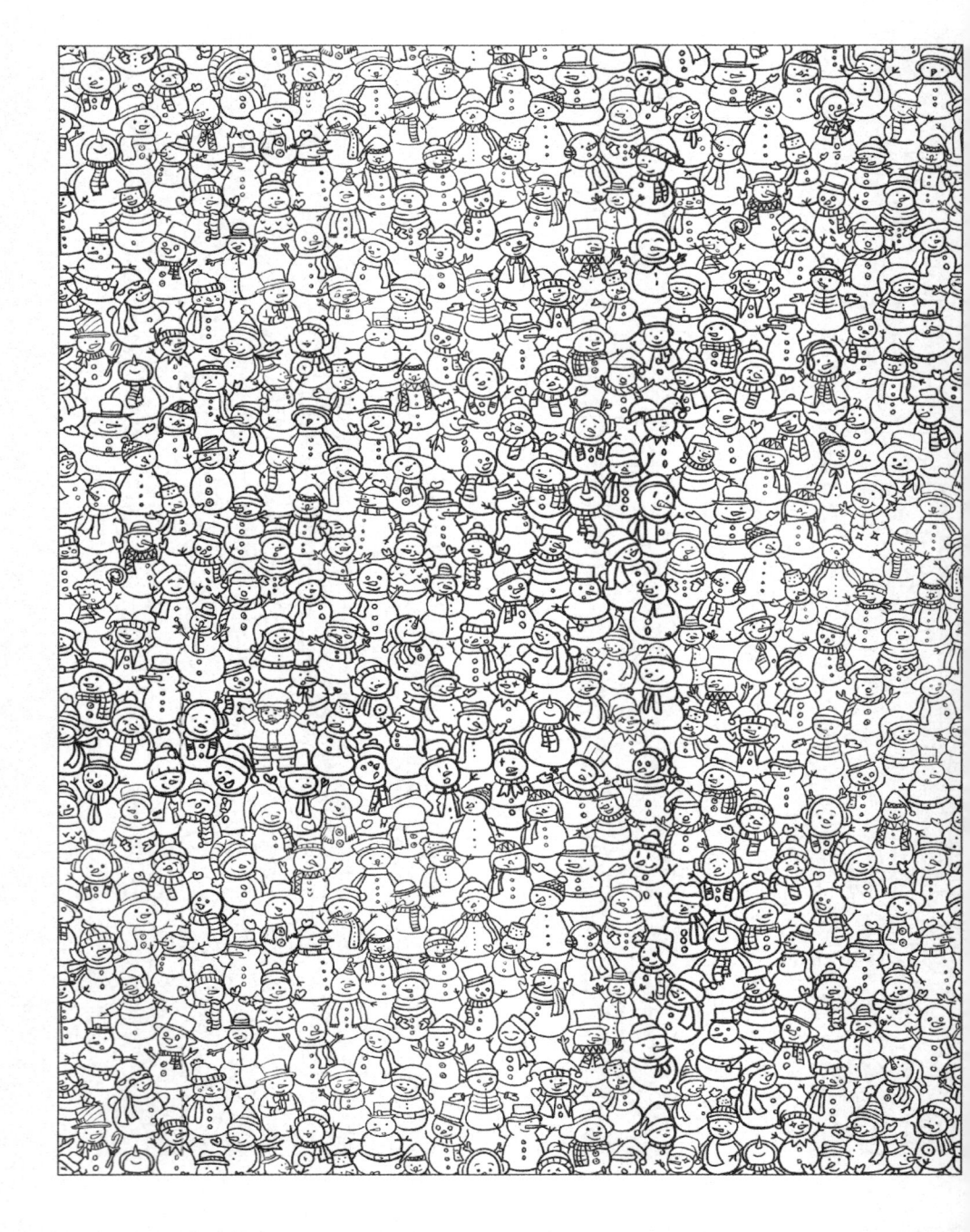

Search and Find

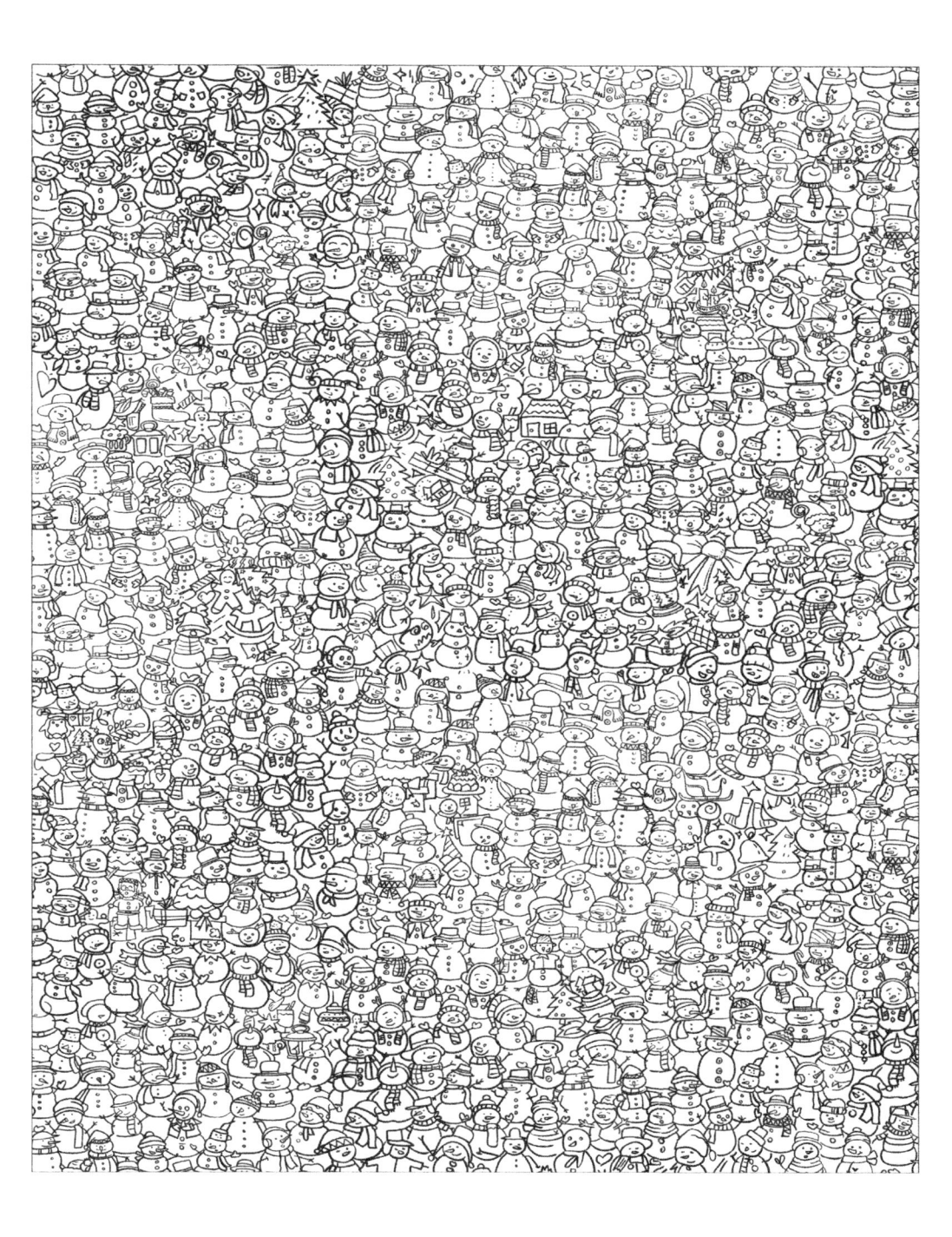

Solutions

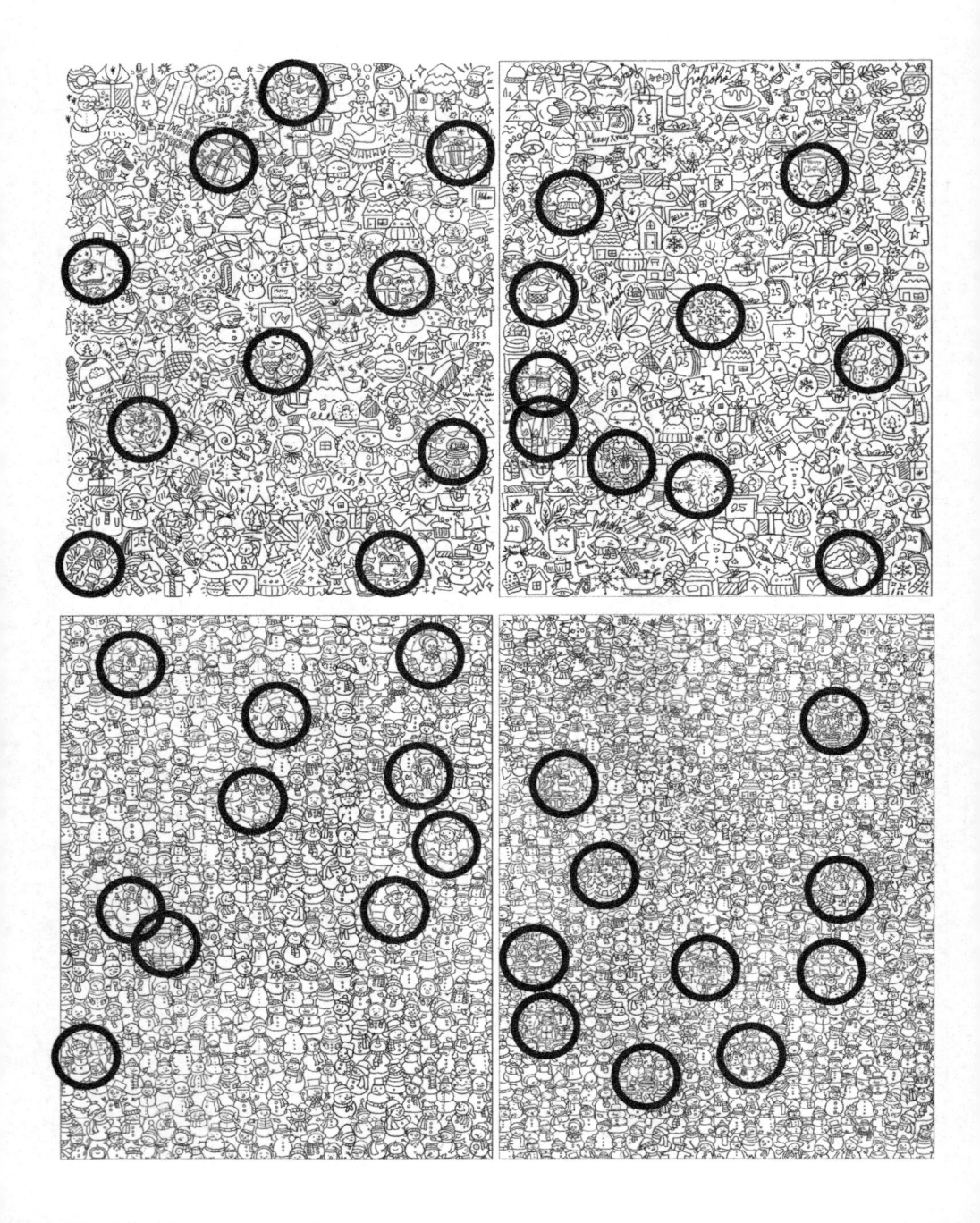

Printed in Great Britain
by Amazon